THE EXALTED HEROINE AND THE
TRIUMPH OF ORDER

The Exalted Heroine and the Triumph of Order

Class, Women and Religion in the English Novel, 1740–1800

K. G. Hall

Barnes & Noble Books

© K. G. Hall 1993

First published in Great Britain 1993 by
THE MACMILLAN PRESS LTD
Houndmills, Basingstoke, Hampshire RG21 2XS
and London
Companies and representatives
throughout the world

This book is published in Macmillan's *Edinburgh Studies in
Culture and Society* series.
General Editors: John Orr and Colin Nicholson

A catalogue record for this book is available from the British Library.

ISBN 0–333–54939–2

Printed in Great Britain by
Antony Rowe Ltd
Chippenham, Wiltshire

First published in the United States of America 1994 by
BARNES & NOBLE BOOKS
4720 Boston Way
Lanham, MD 20706

Library of Congress Cataloging-in-Publication Data
Hall, K. G., 1949–
The exalted heroine and the triumph of order: class, women, and
religion in the English novel, 1740–1800 / K. G. Hall.
p. cm.
Originally published: Houndmills, Basingstoke, Hampshire:
Macmillan, 1993.
Includes bibliographical references and index.
ISBN 0–389–21001–3
1. English fiction—18th century—History and criticism.   2. Women
and literature—Great Britain—History—18th century.   3. Social
classes in literature.   4. Religion in literature.   5. Heroines in
literature.   I. Title.
PR858.W6H35   1994
823'.609352042—dc20   92–23529
                                                      CIP

Contents

Preface

Eighteenth-century English novels vary in both subject-matter and quality but are now often seen merely as forerunners to the novels of the nineteenth century. Some of the most accomplished writers of nineteenth-century fiction were undoubtedly influenced by their predecessors' work, but it would be a pity to view the eighteenth-century novel solely in this light. Unfortunately many readers who are familiar with the writings of Austen, Dickens, Eliot and others have yet to consider even those eighteenth-century novels which were popular and acclaimed in their day. Outside of universities and colleges, where such works rarely play a major part in the syllabus if they are examined at all, few readers will be acquainted with novels written prior to those of Jane Austen.

The pity of this is that some of the great novels of English literature are thus ignored and a lot of modest – yet very enjoyable – works remain largely unread and obscure. Perhaps if the non-specialist reader could be persuaded to try comparatively well-known and accessible novels such as Fielding's *Joseph Andrews* and Smollett's *Humphry Clinker* then they might be inclined to investigate some of the lesser-known fiction. For example, Graves's *The Spiritual Quixote* should pose no problems for the reader who is prepared to consult the explanatory notes accompanying a modern edition, and it repays that small effort with a piquant mixture of satire, polemic and social history. Similarly, anyone who enjoys Austen's writing will be perfectly at home with Burney's *Evelina*; indeed all of the above novels can be warmly recommended if for no other reason than the fact that they are a 'good read'.

Whilst the present study will mainly be of interest to students of literature and the sociology of literature, I have tried to make it comprehensible to anyone curious about the eighteenth-century novel. My approach is informed by sociology and Marxist thought but proposes no grand theory; however, I hope that it has something to offer those interested in the specific novels discussed and those who simply require some information about the background to eighteenth-century English fiction. As the title implies, the main themes are the condition of women and their opportunities for social advancement, real and fictitious, and the maintenance of social order in the face of socio-economic change. During this era a new conception of women – largely created by the novelists and based on the new-found leisure and affluence of the few – gradually came to the fore. The disestablished Anglican Church began to experience a decline, Methodism attracted an increasing number of adherents, and republicanism found favour with some sections of the emerging middle class: the relative social stability maintained throughout the century was certainly far from inevitable.

The book is divided into two parts. In the first there is a consideration of the relationship between literature and ideology, and a chapter which surveys literary realism, the fiction reading/purchasing public, and authorial intention and technique. In the second part I discuss seven individual novels in some detail. The works considered are: Samuel Richardson's *Pamela* (1740); Sarah Fielding's *David Simple* (1744); Henry Fielding's *Amelia* (1751); Oliver Goldsmith's *The Vicar of Wakefield* (1766); Richard Graves's *The Spiritual Quixote* (1773); Fanny Burney's *Evelina* (1778); Robert Bage's *Hermsprong* (1796). These particular novels were chosen because they deal with one or more of the areas which I wished to examine, but I believe that they are representative of the fiction of the period.

My overall purpose has been to give a literary and sociological reading of class, women, and religion in eighteenth-century prose-fiction; to this end I have sought to place the works in their social context, and to consider authorial attitudes towards women and female emancipation, social order, and the role of religion in public and private life.

Part One

Part One

Literature and Ideology

1
Literature and Ideology

Throughout this study the term 'ideology' is used to refer to forms of thought and rhetoric which present the interests of a particular group as the interests of the majority, the nation, or the whole community. As Miliband suggests, Marx and Engels saw ideology as 'precisely the attempt to "universalize" and give "ideal" form to what are no more than limited, class-bound ideas and interests: it is in this sense that they use the word "ideology" pejoratively, as meaning a false representation of reality'.[1] This is not to say that ideologies are always cynically constructed and employed by one class to deceive and manipulate another. The most sincere exponents and believers of a particular ideology often belong to the class which that ideology represents. However, rhetoricians and others from various backgrounds usually appear to lend their pens, voices, and physical might to the promotion of specific ideologies.

I do not wish to suggest that every component of an ideology, or every fictional piece markedly influenced by an ideology, is unavoidably false. Certain ideas and claims may well be true or partly true; nevertheless, the overall picture derived from an ideology will be distorted if only by virtue of the fact that it universalises that which is not truly universal.

So, ideologies are not merely fantasies or aggregations of tendentious lies. Indeed they may, in some instances, constitute the most enlightened and perceptive understanding of human thought and action then attainable: this is possible because ideologies are always generated by social reality. They are not, however, simply straightforward reflections of reality, but partial and incomplete attempts to apprehend and explain reality. Thus an ideology mediates between actual human practices and understanding of the nature of those practices. It is in the process of trying to perceive, interpret and represent reality that distortion occurs, sometimes unwittingly and sometimes as a result of prior intention.

As ideologies play a dynamic role in the relations between human beings, they are usually susceptible to revision and development, according to changing social conditions. However, the need to fulfil particular functions ensures that ideologies typically share some constant features. For example, overtly political ideologies offer some explanation of the past and present, a blueprint for the future, and a statement of the goals and values deemed important by the promoters of the ideology. Such ideologies typically provide more or less comprehensive guidance for action and seek to draw support and legitimation from all or most members of a given society.[2] In this way, political ideologues and activists try to establish the universality of their own perspectives.

The manner in which ideologies are created and transmitted will obviously vary according to the general conditions pertaining to a given society; suffice to state that the proponents of an ideology will almost certainly try to utilise whatever means are available to propagate, establish and maintain their own Weltanschauung. Some classes are in a better position to do this than others, hence Marx's claim that 'The ideas of the ruling class are in every epoch the ruling ideas, i.e. the class which is the ruling *material* force of society, is at the same time its ruling *intellectual* force'.[3]

It is my contention that each of the novels considered below paints an ideological picture of the social relations and conditions existing in England at the time of their writing. This can be illustrated by reference to the actual socio-political structure of eighteenth-century England. Although I do not wish to claim that all of the authors shared the same background and perspective, it is undeniable that there is a considerable convergence between them in their social origins, their general view of society, and the concerns which are prominent in their texts. All were from bourgeois or gentry families, all subscribed to a greater or lesser extent to essentially bourgeois ideals, and all demonstrated some adherence to, or at least respect for, Christianity, usually in its Anglican form. Every novelist here makes some criticisms of the aristocracy, mainly through attacks upon the supposed lechery of male peers; yet all, with the exception of the Fieldings, go on to display a good deal of admiration for that class.

The salient concerns appearing in the novels are as follows: status and social mobility; marriage and female virtue; social order; personal morality; the role of the Anglican Church. The homogeneity of content is hardly surprising, not because literature can be said to reflect society in any, unequivocal way, but rather because, in addition to the convergence mentioned above, it is easy to see why authors should choose to write about topics deemed relevant by the bourgeoisie, gentry and aristocracy. The former constituted a large part of the reading public; this public was eager to read novels which dealt with social issues of contemporary interest. The authors were likely to have shared the interests of their readers and, moreover, simply could not afford to ignore the tastes of potential customers if they wished to sell their novels. As patronage in the literary sphere had gone into decline from the early part of the century, novelistic success became dependent upon the ability of the author to make his or her work appeal to a wider social grouping than had hitherto been influential in the arts.[4]

The fact that writers had to *attract* readers has implications for the literary form and thus for the transmission of ideology through the novel. Authors were not in the position of, for example, clergymen, whose sermons and directives were frequently sanctioned by considerable spiritual and secular authority. They did not have the captive audience which many – particularly rural – Anglican ministers had as a result of both metaphysical fear on the part of parishioners, and material threats from pro-Anglican members of the ruling class. Even the most consciously didactic writers such as Richardson had to be able to offer something more than a list of instructions and proscriptions. Not that spiritual guidance and religious discussion were unpopular during the period if the number of religious works published is anything to go by. Watt points out that the majority of books published during the century were of this type, but goes on to add, 'the number of religious publication does not deem to have increased in proportion either to the growth of the population or to the sales of other types of reading matter. Further, the public for religious reading seems to have been rather independent of that for secular literature'.[5] Indeed it seems likely that those inclined to purchase sermons and other religiously oriented works might well be disdainful of prose-fiction, in the same way that the reader of 'romances' would probably not be excited by theological exposition. A didactically-motivated writer would surely be inclined to try to influence as many readers as possible, and in particular those in need of moral guidance. In this instance the morally-deprived readers would be identified as those who read romances rather than religious works; therefore the writer who could pursue a didactic purpose and yet still draw readers from this expanding section of the reading public would stand to achieve both moral and commercial success. Samuel Richardson's *Pamela* is perhaps the best example of such a success; nevertheless the attempt to provide some form of moral or spiritual teaching in a manner which would attract and entertain a large audience is a common feature of many eighteenth-century novels.

There are some crucial differences in the way in which ideology appears in fiction as opposed to religious teaching. The latter, whether delivered from the pulpit or transcribed in book or pamphlet form, faced several problems which the novelist could avoid. The Anglican Church sought to convey its message to an extremely heterogeneous audience, but teaching pitched at the level of discourse which was readily available to all would inevitably be tedious to the educated listener or reader, whilst the ideological nature of its content would tend to be more explicit and thus obvious even to many of those who had little formal education. If, on the other hand, religious claims and explanations were stated in accordance with the more rigorous and/or esoteric canons of philosophy and theology, then they would undoubtedly have been comprehensible to only a small section of the Church's potential audience. It may be argued that these obstacles could have been surmounted by providing simplistic sermons for the uneducated, and more sophisticated theological discussion for the cultured via printed matter. To some extent this strategy was adopted; additionally an enormous number of religious tracts were produced and distributed (gratis) in an effort to inculcate religiosity amongst the working class.[6] However there was a further problem for those who would spread the gospel; they frequently found a fair measure of apathy regarding religious matters – and this lack of interest was not confined to any one class.

In contrast, the novelist did not have to produce works which would appeal to such a variety of people. The reading/purchasing public, notwithstanding the socio-economic diversity amongst those who constituted it, was a considerably more homogeneous group in terms of education, economic position, status and values than the audience envisaged by the Church for *its* message. So whilst the novelist had to attract readers, he or she did not have have to deal with the problem of addressing those with little or no education or the classically learned. The latter educationally-élite readers were, with some exceptions, little interested in contemporary fictional writing, especially in the early part of the century. However, the middle class, the bulk of the reading public, possessed both the economic and educational means necessary for the novel to flourish. The author's task was to attract, entertain and (particularly after

Richardson) instruct this growing section of the public; yet in contrast to the clergy the novelist could promise something new in both form and content, and present the whole in a diverting manner.

Perhaps the most striking difference between the presentation of ideology in religion as opposed to prose-fiction hinges on the fact that Anglican teaching was overtly dictatorial (at least as far as the majority of its audience was concerned), and designed to inspire obedience both spiritual and secular with the weapon of fear. The use of religious and civil sanctions had been successful in the past, but it became increasingly ineffective as the century progressed. And, far from ensuring obedience to the Church and its allies, it contributed to the long-term decline in Anglican influence over the population. Put simply, the Church did not match its ideology and practices to changing social conditions, but continued to demand duty, obedience and respect from reluctant, then antagonistic, and finally uninterested people.

Much fictional prose was essentially supportive towards the religious and secular authority of the day, but did not usually try to direct its audience in such an uncompromising way. Instead it might be argued that literary ideologues tried to reinforce certain aspects of the material and spiritual status quo by creating the more imaginative and multi-dimensional means of influence exemplified in the novel. For if religious functionaries could be said to follow the mode of teaching associated with *The Book of the Covenant* and other Old Testament writings, wherein obedience is demanded and little or no explanation offered, then the didactic, Anglican-oriented novelist might be seen as pursuing Christ's parable style of instruction.[7] The parable is a form which implicitly recognises the need to capture the attention of a *voluntary* audience as a precondition for instruction, and indeed some eighteenth-century English novels resemble nothing so much as parables expanded and artistically developed.

One recurring issue which surfaces in all of the novels discussed below is the question of how the individual can be properly integrated within his or her society. It is understandable that this should be a constant theme in fiction given the advances made by the ideology of individualism, and the varied opportunities for social mobility present during the greater part of the century. The ideology of individualism posited the allegedly inevitable opposition between the 'individual' and 'society', yet in practice it was clearly felt that integration was both desirable and necessary. For our authors, as for others sympathetic to the bourgeoisie, the best kind of integration

was achieved by upward mobility, and this became a common literary solution to the practical problems posed in the eighteenth-century novel.

The specifically bourgeois views which came to be absorbed by
the gentry and the aristocracy throughout the century centre around
the idea of individualism; this ideology represented beliefs and values which were in sharp contrast to those which had dominated
medieval Europe. As noted by Weber et al. the ideology and practice of economic individualism occurred only after the Reformation
and the rise of radical-Protestant theology; even so, this development was confined to a handful of countries, England being the
prime example.[8] Tawney contrasts the two sets of beliefs when he
remarks:

> The law of nature had been invoked by medieval writers as a
> moral restraint upon economic self-interest. By the seventeenth
> century a significant change had taken place. 'Nature' had come to
> connote not divine ordinance, but human appetites, and natural
> rights were invoked by the individualism of the age as a reason
> why self-interest should be given free play.[9]

Mészáros argues that the decline of the Aristotelian world-view
and the increasing preoccupation with individual freedom which
preceded the flowering of economic individualism 'was due . . . to
the dynamic development of the capitalistic relations of production
which required the universal extension of "liberty" to every single
individual so that he could enter into "free contractual relations"
with other individuals, for the purpose of selling and alienating
everything that belongs to him, including his own 'labour power'.[10]
This is not to deny the role of, for example, the 'Protestant ethic' in
the process of change, but rather to underline the fact that it was
clearly related to material developments. For as Mészáros points
out, 'It is by no means accidental that individual liberty as a political
and moral ideal is absent from the ancient world, and appears only
with the High Renaissance. When "direct dependence on nature" is
a general concern of a particular community, aspirations to a distinct
form of individual liberty can only be expressed marginally'.[11]

In eighteenth-century England the most important statement of
individualism was that formulated by John Locke, whose political
theory, as Tawney notes, completely contradicted earlier doctrines.[12]
C. B. Macpherson has termed Locke's theory 'possessive individual-

ism', as it is based on the idea of the individual as a 'proprietor of his own person or capacities'.[13] This conception of individuals artificially detaches them from the context in which they become – and exist as – human beings. But according to Locke this supposed isolation is to be seen as an aspect of freedom; Macpherson continues, 'The human essence is freedom from dependence on the wills of others, and freedom is a function of possession'.[14]

It is all very well to speak of an individual as 'owning' his or her person, capacities and whatever else they can acquire by the exercise of those capacities, but this notion implies much that Locke disregarded. For as Macpherson states, the bourgeois concept of property includes the right to 'dispose of, to exchange, to alienate'.[15] With the proviso that one cannot dispose of one's own life (seen as the property of God), this means that one can alienate one's property by selling one's labour power.[16] The fact that the majority of individuals in Locke's society were forced to alienate their property in this way does not appear to have concerned him; yet this being the case, how could these wage-labourers be considered free from 'dependence on the wills of others'? Therefore, as Macpherson contends, the process of selling one's labour-power for a bare subsistence wage (all that labourers could ever expect according to Locke) ensures that wage-labourers *necessarily* alienate their lives and liberty.[17] Locke's lack of concern on this point is less surprising when one considers that he also claimed that unemployment arose from the 'moral depravity' of the unemployed; that labourers were incapable of any sort of political action except in the most extraordinary circumstances, and that proper administration of the poor did not involve providing them with minimal subsistence, but rather preventing them from suffering so grievously that they might attempt 'armed revolt'.[18]

Perhaps the most far-reaching implication of Locke's theory in the present context is that stated by Macpherson as follows: 'If it is labour, a man's absolute property, which justifies appropriation and creates value, the individual right of appropriation overrides any moral claims of the society. The traditional view that property and labour were social functions, and that ownership of property involved social obligations, is thereby undermined'.[19]

Changing material conditions and the development of the ideas outlined above resulted in the gradual rise of individualism during the eighteenth century. Stone concludes that by the early part of the century 'complete identification had been made between the pursuit of gratification by the individual and the welfare of the public'.[20]

In Marx's famous *Introduction to a Critique of Political Economy* he discusses the ideological conception of the 'solitary producer' as used in fiction (Defoe's *Robinson Crusoe*), and later by the economists Adam Smith and David Ricardo. Marx observes that the model arises from an 'anticipation of "bourgeois society" ', and remarks, 'The individual in this society of free competition seems to be rid of the natural ties etc. which made him an appurtenance of a particular, limited aggregation of human beings in previous historical epochs'.[21] As Marx goes on to point out, the further back one delves into history the more dependent upon some form of collectivity does the individual appear to be. The perception of the individual and individualism which eventually held sway amongst eighteenth-century ideologists was itself historically conditioned; furthermore their attempt to understand 'man' by supposing their vision of human characteristics to hold good for any historical period underlines the vanity and sterility of such ahistorical speculation.

As noted above, one consequence of individualism was that many eighteenth-century British theorists came to view the individual and society as separate and opposing forces. Regardless of such ideology, however, there is no such thing as society or individuals, if by these terms one means that they are entities which can justifiably be supposed to exist apart from one another; additionally it should be clear that no 'society' oppresses the 'individual'. Avineri, examining Marx's view of the matter, sums it up nicely when he writes, 'The phenomenon so described is the domination of some individuals by other individuals, with the latter aided and abetted by ideologies of the "common good" '.[22]

As individualism gradually became a dominant trend in eighteenth-century English philosophy it is not surprising to find some evidence for its penetration into the novel. However, whilst all of the works examined below contain some material influenced by individualism, they all display a definite concern with the problem of individual–social integration.[23] The questions which occur most frequently in the texts are: what is possible, and what is desirable? None of the writers favourably portray the sort of extreme individualism which, as Watt notes, can be found in Defoe's work.[24] Furthermore there is a marked difference in the extent to which particular authors accept the premises of individualism; Henry Fielding, Graves and Goldsmith show little of the enthusiasm for an individualistic society that can be detected in some of the other writers, as the former remain influenced by a somewhat organicist conception of social organisation.[25] No writer discussed here endorsed the kind of unbridled individualism advocated by Locke and others.

The term 'class' was little used during the eighteenth century; given the ubiquity of what George describes as 'minute social distinctions' it appears that the social hierarchy was seen as one of status differences based primarily – but not solely – on wealth; these differences were expressed in the notions of 'rank', 'station', 'degree' and so on.[26] Reference to social aggregations was conveyed by terms such as 'the quality', 'the gentry', 'the middling sort', 'the lower orders' and 'the poor'. That there were groups who shared a more or less similar position in English society according to land ownership, wealth, etc. was undoubtedly recognised. However the somewhat superficial heterogeneity within such groups, combined with those real differences that existed, seems to have encouraged an essentially individual-oriented attitude towards the assessment of position within the social hierarchy. Therefore the manner in which any person's social standing would be determined by eighteenth-century contemporaries is more individualistic than is consistent with class analysis.

This individualising tendency finds its way into the novels, which typically present only a narrow range of social types and activity in any detail. In the main the novels deal with the experiences of the bourgeoisie and, to a lesser extent, the ruling class: that is with the relations (on an individual and personalised level) existing amongst the bourgeoisie, and between them and the ruling class. Workers and the poor (often one and the same) do not, despite noteworthy exceptions such as Pamela and Moll Flanders, usually play a prominent part in eighteenth-century novels. Likewise the aristocracy, although often central to a plot as the representatives of all that is wicked or as exemplars of goodness (and the means of upward mobility), receive far less attention than their bourgeois counterparts. Thus the protagonists and scenarios of the novel in this period do not usually facilitate consideration of the relations between the ruling class and bourgeoisie to their common social inferiors. The 'lower orders' may make an appearance as the object of fear, mirth, or pious exhortation, but their presence is most frequently notable for its absence. In short, the middle-class nature of the novel is partly illustrated by the fact that it aimed, primarily, to portray the bourgeoisie.

Where the existence of distinct and competing groups is acknowledged in the novels, the conservative bias of the opinions put forward by major characters can be easily demonstrated. However, the most salient assumption regarding rank which colours these works, is that individuals – whatever their social, political or economic differences – can, should, and invariably do live in harmony as contented members of an inevitably hierarchical, well-ordered society. Social conflict is usually viewed as unnatural, unnecessary and – significantly – transitory. At the root of any social disturbance one will find individual troublemakers and villains who dupe the unwise and intemperate; thus conflict allegedly stems from those who will not (or cannot) control vicious impulses and passions which arise from greed, envy and malice. None of the literary portrayals of conflict which one might identify as class conflict are ever portrayed as rational, inevitable or justifiable.

Throughout the period considered, the feminine ideal employed in the English novel showed little variation; heroines are, with few exceptions, possessed of beauty and good sense combined with chasteness and modesty. Above all they are properly deferential to men, whether father, guardian, suitor or husband. The ideal remains fairly constant regardless of the heroine's social origins; thus Pamela, in spite of her humble upbringing, shares virtually all of the positive feminine qualities displayed by Fielding's Amelia and Goldsmith's Sophia, who are from gentry and lower-bourgeois families respectively. These characteristics are in turn possessed by heroines of aristocratic origin, such as Bage's Caroline and Burney's Evelina; the examples can be multiplied. Perhaps the most notable heroines who do not conform to this pattern in the eighteenth-century novel are Moll Flanders and Roxana, but then they are not, as Defoe himself made clear, meant to be viewed as models for imitation or admiration.

Although the dominant ideological picture of women which informs these works is drawn from largely bourgeois ideals, this does not mean that there was any substantial disagreement between the bourgeoisie and the aristocracy in their views on women. It is true that some of the writers criticise lecherous males belonging to the quality, but this does not indicate a generally critical attitude towards social superiors on the part of the bourgeoisie. Nor does it stand as evidence that members of the aristocracy were typically engaged in debauchery and utterly opposed to bourgeois moralising. As Stone suggests:

By the end of the eighteenth century a consensus was emerging about the ideal education for women of the landed classes and for the higher ranks of the bourgeoisie. She was neither the frivolous, party-going, neglectful mother and possibly adulterous wife of the aristocracy, nor the middle-class intellectual blue-stocking who challenged and threatened men on their own ground of the classics. She was a well-informed and motivated woman with the educational training and the internalized desire to devote her life partly to pleasing her husband and providing him with friendship and intelligent companionship, partly to the efficient supervision of the servants and domestic arrangements; and partly to educating her children in ways appropriate for their future.[27]

The ideal of feminine virtue displayed in novels, then, was an indication of a more concrete, broad consensus developing amongst the middle and upper classes. Thus the exemplary female characters who appear in the novel represent the ideal produced by members of those classes.

It is significant that almost all of the paragons of womanhood who are described in the works under examination play little or no part in the world of work and, typically, make no contribution to 'household' economy. Adburgham points out that 'As the eighteenth century advanced, the unmarried woman of a family ceased to be an economical asset in her capacity of spinner, weaver, and seamstress, because less of these labours were done in the home. Also, it was becoming fashionable for gentlewomen to leave all household tasks to the servants'.[28] And Stone, writing on female education during the period, argues 'It presupposed a growing number of women wholly withdrawn from productive work and with a great deal of enforced leisure on their hands.[29]

However, women from the middle and upper classes constituted a small proportion of females in England; the majority of women, who continued to work in one capacity or another, rarely held much interest for the novelists. When ordinary working women appear in their writings they most often play the part of faithful servant or disreputable, 'low' character; consequently they are not usually attributed the individuality associated with their socio-economic superiors.

Discussing female sexuality and its relation to class in the eighteenth-century novel, LeGates has argued that 'The dichotomy is not between the chaste bourgeoisie and the licentious lady, but between the virtuous woman of the upper classes (whether by merit or birth) and the loose woman of the lower orders (whether by choice or circumstance).[30] In fact the most significant division between these fictional females rests upon whether a character is chaste and modest or unchaste and immodest, *regardless of class position or origin*. Most of the heroines do not come from the aristocracy, gentry or upper bourgeoisie (that is, the upper class), but rather from the middle or lower-middle class. Heroes tend to be of a higher status or class than heroines and thus literary romances conform to B.'s idea – shared by Johnson et al. – that women are 'ennobled' when they marry an appropriate partner. Throughout the century it was considered (from the lower-middle class upwards) to be disgusting for a woman to marry a social inferior, and so this literary convention is hardly surprising. Fielding disregards it in *Amelia* but in this he was atypical. If it were not the case that heroines had humbler origins than their male counterparts then one of the major themes of the eighteenth-century English novel would have been lost: the theme is, quite simply, the upward social mobility of the heroine via marriage. So,many heroines may ultimately be accepted into the upper classes (like Pamela or Sophia) but they are not initially 'of the upper classes'; given this, it is misleading to claim that virtue can be seen as a solely upper-class characteristic.

One might argue that no eighteenth-century novel was complete without one or two clergymen; Anglican ministers play a prominent part in five of the seven works considered here (*Pamela* and *David Simple* show them in minor roles only) as they do in many English novels of the period. S. C. Carpenter, discussing this phenomenon, states that: 'The clergy of eighteenth-century fiction are a numerous and most interesting company, and no doubt sketches from life', but I think that one must be somewhat sceptical about this proposition.[31] It is true that there is some variation in the presentation of ministers, and that writers such as Henry Fielding do not always cast them in a favourable light. Nevertheless for every haughty, negligent or uncharitable clergyman shown in fiction one can find a good many more who approximate to an idealised model; even Bage, who created a clerical villain, was not above using the 'benevolent clergyman' stereotype. This broadly consisted of a minister who was anything from poor to middling (with a slight tendency towards the former perhaps), usually middle-aged, and possessing all of those qualities which could be of service to – or be approved by – the heroine and hero of the piece. Such characters typically have an unlimited supply of good sense and acute judgement (for giving sagacious advice), augmented with a strong sense of moral and parochial duty, courage, and tenderness. Additional common traits include patriotism, a preference for passivity and piety (and thus the maintenance of the status quo), and monarchism. Last, but perhaps most importantly, these worthies tend to have a detailed grasp of the requirements of propriety: a useful faculty for those charged with guiding young lovers.

Through the use of such characters the novelists seek to support religion, and it is by the same means – with less favourable models – that they offer criticism of some Anglican ministers. Whether praising or criticising, the writers invariably dealt with the Church by creating good or bad individual clergymen; the institutional aspect of Anglicanism was largely ignored. Even so, in some instances the novelists do shed light on attitudes towards the Church's representatives, simply by constructing a model of what would pass for an honest, dutiful and spiritual minister. Few of the writers saw anything wrong with the fact the clergy expounded political doctrines, or that they were – given the chance – deeply involved with the wealthy and powerful, for example. Moreover it is significant in itself that all of the authors considered Anglican ministers to be of sufficient interest to merit inclusion in their novels; such characters often play, in fiction as in fact, an important role in the action.

Apart from Anglicanism the most important religious ideas which find a place in the novels here examined are Puritanism and Methodism; they will be considered in the chapters on *Pamela* and *The Spiritual Quixote* respectively.

2
The Novel and Society
1740-1800

THE NOVEL AND REALISM

As noted above, the ideology of individualism became increasingly influential in eighteenth-century England; the driving force behind it was the prosperous bourgeoisie which emerged as a powerful class throughout the century. One of the major cultural products associated with this class is the novel; it is not suggested here that the novel suddenly appeared as a finished form in the period, but rather that the gradual formation of the bourgeoisie as a distinct economic group in the preceding centuries, and their creation, articulation and transmission of – especially – individualist ideology, provided the necessary intellectual scenario, and indeed the actual reading public, which made possible the process which Ian Watt has termed 'the rise of the novel'.

Watt notes the connection between the appearance of the bourgeoisie and the subsequent development of the novel, and goes on to argue that 'formal realism', which he takes to be the defining characteristic of the novel, itself only occurs once individualism has begun to challenge pre-capitalist notions of tradition. He writes, 'from the Renaissance onwards, there was a growing tendency for individual experience to replace collective tradition as the ultimate arbiter of reality; and this transition would seem to constitute an important part of the general cultural background to the rise of the novel'.[1]

According to Watt, literary forms prior to the novel not only rely upon reference to literary tradition to establish truth, but are also dependent upon plots drawn from past history or fable.[2] He continues,

> Defoe and Richardson are the first great writers in our literature who did not take their plots from mythology, history, legend, or previous literature. In this they differ from Chaucer, Spenser,

16

Shakespeare, and Milton, for instance, who, like the writers of Greece and Rome, habitually used traditional plots; and who did so, in the last analysis, because they accepted the general premise of their times that, since Nature is essentially complete and un-changing, its records, whether scriptural, legendary, or historical, constitute a definitive repertoire of human experience.[3]

The uniqueness of individual experience on which the novel con-centrates entails that the novelist continually aims to show that which is both particular and new; thus the novel necessarily contra-dicts the assumptions which had hitherto informed literature.[4] The novelist typically seeks to portray 'particular people in particular circumstances', and to give a detailed account of persons and their environment; additionally, there is a tendency for the novelist to use proper rather than 'type' names and to draw upon contemporary (or near-contemporary) life. Moreover, language in the novel is primarily employed in a referential, and not poetically decorative, manner.[5]

Watt sees the focus upon the individual in the novel as a manifes-tation of the increasing interest in – and changing definition of – realism in eighteenth-century England, both in philosophy and lit-erature. Regarding philosophy, he states, 'Modern realism . . . begins from the position that *truth can be discovered by the individual through his senses*.'[6] But whilst Watt wishes to suggest a connection between philosophical and literary realism, he does not want to imply that the former causes the latter, nor does he suppose that literary realism adheres to 'specialized tenets' derived from philosophical realism.[7] However, he does maintain that the change in literature outlined above 'was analogous to the rejection of universals and the emphasis on particulars which characterizes philosophical realism'; moreover, what is significant about the novel in this context is that it is in keeping with the general temper of realist thought.[8] The fact that eighteenth-century novelists and philosophers concentrated upon the individual in this way can be explained by reference to the wider cultural background and, for Watt, their shared aim: 'the production of what purports to be an authentic account of the actual experiences of individuals'.[9]

However implausible the modern reader may find the writings of eighteenth-century English novelists, there is little doubt that the authors themselves (excluding the later writers of 'Gothic' and other fantastic tales) were attempting to avoid the incredible. Just what is deemed realistic will obviously vary historically and geographically: nevertheless, both eighteenth-century authors and readers saw the innovative writing of Richardson, Henry Fielding and others as far more realistic than previous literature. All of the writers discussed here (with the exception of Bage) made claims for the realism of their novels, although this is not to say that they all adhered to exactly the same conception of realism, nor does it entail that realism was the only major principle guiding the construction of the novels. For example, the psychologically-oriented approach to character found in *Pamela* is largely absent from the other works examined, Burney's *Evelina* being the most similar in that it employs psychological drama-tisation via the subjectivity of the main character. The realism of the novels is rather more dependent upon their plausibility as credible stories told in a manner which does not strain the reader's sense of verisimilitude too severely. In each case the author has made some effort to avoid the use of stereotypes and to offer authentic and individualised characters involved in circumstances peculiar to them but – at least theoretically – possible for other people.

Didacticism was as important as realism for these writers, and they clearly did not see themselves as simply producing credible fictions, for their works include moral exhortation and (often) the claim that moral teaching was the main purpose of writing fiction. It is important to remember this point when assessing the English prose-fiction of this period because, as Tompkins has observed, for writers, readers and critics 'the function of the novel was explicitly educational and . . . its main business was to inculcate morality by example'; consequently, novels were expected to 'always show life subservient to moral law'.[10] Not all of the novelists of the age viewed their task with the seriousness implied by these strictures, but it is noteworthy that even Defoe – whose *Moll Flanders* and *Roxana* were probably read mainly for their accounts of loose-living and criminality – went through the motions of claiming a moral purpose for his novels.

If the realism associated with the eighteenth-century novel repre-sented a break with earlier forms of literature, the concern of the authors to make a moral point in their fiction illustrates a degree of continuity with legend, mythology, biblical and folk tales. All of these forms typically provided both a story and a moral, the latter being equally, if not more, important; yet these previous modes of expressing fictional creativity did not conform to formal realism. And, in the absence of the comparatively rigorous criteria governing what might be taken as realistic in the novel, it is almost certainly easier to produce a story which perfectly illustrates a moral point. If, however, a writer seeks to construct a fiction which adheres to formal realism and also articulates a moral message, there is likely to be some tension between the two aims. In eighteenth-century novels any clash between these two was usually resolved by the preservation of the moral of the story at the expense of the realism; in this way, *pace* Benjamin, the novel usually did have, 'counsel' for its readers.[11]

AUTHORS AND READERS

Having briefly considered realism and didacticism, we can turn to the question of whether or not the eighteenth-century novel can justly be termed 'bourgeois'. This label is usually applied with reference to one or more of the following: the author's social origins; the class composition of the reading public to whom the work was directed; the actual content of the novel – that is, does the novel articulate what are essentially bourgeois ideas and concerns?

For the first of these criteria one can cite the figures compiled by Raymond Williams; these indicate that during the period 1680–1730, thirteen out of nineteen English writers came from the professional (and thus middle) class, four from the ranks of merchants, tradesmen and craftsmen (lower-middle class), and two from the nobility and gentry. Between 1730 and 1780, eleven out of twenty-five had professional origins; two came from the nobility; additionally there were four tradesmen, four farmers, three craftsmen and one merchant. From 1780 to 1830, twenty-five out of fifty-seven writers had professional origins; one was from the nobility and eight were from the gentry; there were also nine merchants, five tradesmen, five craftsmen, two poor farmers and one labourer. To summarise, in the first period seventeen of the nineteen writers had middle class origins; in the second period twenty-three of the twenty-five were middle class; in the third period forty-five out of fifty-seven were from the middle class. This preponderance of writers from the middle class does indicate the extent to which that class can be seen as the dominant force in the production of prose-fiction during the eighteenth-century.[12]

The social origins of the writers included in this story were bourgeois in four cases and gentry in three. Samuel Richardson's father was a joiner who employed three apprentices; prior to this the men of Richardson's family had been yeomen for several generations. Richardson himself was apprenticed to a printer because his father could not afford to place him in the Church; however, he went on to become a master printer, married his employer's daughter, and was very successful. As Eaves and Kimpel observe, 'Richardson's life was that of a conventional middle class businessman'.[13] 'In contrast, Edmund Fielding – father of Sarah and Henry – was a colonel and (reputedly) a 'Hanoverian rake'.[14] Both he and his wife were from gentry families (his family having claim to greater nobility, her family being financially solvent), therefore Sarah and Henry can be seen as having gentry origins. Richard Graves, who spent his working life within the Anglican Church as a rector, was the son of a country squire.[15]

Oliver Goldsmith's father was an Anglican curate who owned a seventy-acre farm; Goldsmith also wanted to take orders but was rejected. Prior to writing, Goldsmith did some menial jobs, but was mostly engaged in the middle class occupations of tutor and physician.[16] Fanny Burney's father was a member of the upper bourgeoisie; he was variously an organist a fairly lucrative occupation at £100 per annum), a composer and music teacher, and then a music master for the fashionable. He was also a prominent music historian. Fanny, who was schooled in Paris, did not have to work for her living.[17] Robert Bage was a papermaker, like his father; apart from having his own business he was – according to Scott – involved in an unsuccessful attempt to establish an iron 'manufactory'. Bage's letters frequently display the concerns of the businessman and contain a number of references to the wage-demands of his employees: these never failed to alarm him.[18]

Using the class position of the authors' fathers, four can be placed within the middle class and three within the gentry. If, however, one focuses upon the individual writer's relation to the means of production as the sole criterion here, then there is a strong case for concluding that all of them were essentially middle class. None of the cited authors from gentry families actually lived primarily from income derived from land.

The reading public for the eighteenth-century English novel was mainly middle class in composition. As Williams suggests,

It is from the 1690s that the growth of a new kind of middle class reading public becomes evident, in direct relation to the growth of a new kind of middle class defined as merchants, tradesmen, shopkeepers and administrative and clerical workers. New forms of reading, in the newspaper, the periodical and the magazine, account for the major expansion, and behind them comes the novel, in close relation to this particular public.[19]

And, as Watt points out, whilst the reading public grew during the eighteenth-century, 'it still did not formally extend much further down the social scale than to tradesmen and shopkeepers, with the important exception of the more favoured apprentices and indoor servants'.[20] Although a small number of those below the middle class may have had the necessary skill, leisure, and access to books required in order to read novels, the vast majority of the population clearly did not.

Burke, states Watt, thought that the reading public numbered around 80 000 (out of a population of 6 000 000+) in the 1790s; Hemmings suggests that 'even by the end of the century there may have been no more than 100 000 persons in the country who could read print with any facility', and Williams speculates, 'it seems probable that general literacy did not increase, and may even have declined, in the period between the Restoration and the end of the eighteenth-century'.[21] By all estimates the number of readers was fairly small; smaller still was the number of *book-buyers*. Watt, extrapolating from the sale of the most popular books of the period, concludes that this buying public numbered only 'tens of thousands', and goes on to note the costly nature of books at the time.[22] Consequently, 'The novel in the eighteenth-century was closer to the economic capacity of the middle class additions to the reading public than were many of the established and respectable forms of literature and scholarship, but it was not, strictly speaking, a popular literary form.[23] Hemmings, using the example of an inexpensive edition of *Tom Jones* (six volumes at 3s. each), claims that it 'cost more than a labourer would earn in a week', but most labourers would have though themselves lucky to earn about half of this sum per week.[24] Nevertheless, one can agree with Williams when he writes, 'book-buying was obviously socially limited, and it is very significant that the eighteenth-century public depended, to a considerable extent, on devices of corporate buying', that is, bookclubs and societies, proprietary libraries and so on.[25]

As the middle class were both the major writers and purchasers of novels in the eighteenth-century it is hardly surprising that these works were usually middle class in orientation. Readers above the ranks of the bourgeoisie undoubtedly bought and read some of the novels and – as indicated above – sometimes wrote them; however, they did not constitute the majority of readers or authors. One can accept that some readers below the middle class had access to books owned by their employers, but such people rarely bought novels themselves. Any author who wished to sell his or her work would therefore be unlikely to consider the literary desires of this small and economically insignificant part of the reading public, even if he or she was aware of those desires. Bourgeois authors apparently had little difficulty in deciding what their public wanted, for, as Watt suggests of Defoe and Richardson, 'As middle class London trades-men they had only to consult their own standards of form and content to be sure that what they wrote would appeal to a large audience'.[26] This is, perhaps, something of a simplification, but it is basically correct.

The first two criteria listed above give some credence to the claim that the novel was a bourgeois form, but ultimately it is the third criterion which is the most significant. The social origins and/or class position of any given author are not very important in the present context: as noted previously, one can be an ideologue for a particular class without belonging to that class oneself. This applies just as much to the production of fictional prose as it does to political tracts and the like. It is perfectly possible in principle for an aristo-crat or an artisan to write a bourgeois novel, even though this might be somewhat unusual in practice. The most salient feature of the bourgeois novel is its content: content which is always – regardless of how skilfully or artistically it is handled – an articulation of bourgeois concerns seen from a bourgeois point of view. In this way the bourgeois novel raises middle-class problems to which the au-thor provides middle-class solutions. How far the content of the seven novels discussed here can be said to be bourgeois should become clear in the following chapters.

INTENTION AND TECHNIQUE

In Richardson's preface to the second part of *Pamela* he refers to the success of the original and 'hopes, that the Letters which compose this Part will be found equally written to NATURE avoiding all romantic flights, improbable surprises, and irrational machinery; and the passions are touched, where requisite; and rules, equally *new* and *practicable*, inculcated throughout the whole, for the *general conduct of life*'.[27] Here Richardson is not only claiming that his work is realistic or authentic, but is also enthusiastically advertising its *didactic* nature. The text, which Richardson claimed was based upon a true story which he had heard some years prior to the creation of *Pamela*, is presented as a series of letters written (mainly) by the eponymous heroine. Additional material appears as extracts from the diary or journal which she composes. With the exception of a small part of the text in which Richardson intervenes to move the narrative along, and his drawing of moral conclusions at the close of the first part, there is no overt intrusion by the author *qua* author.[28] Therefore the novel is basically epistolary and told through the subjectivity of Pamela. In addition to the immediacy which one might expect from first-person narrative, Richardson's writing does have a certain dramatic quality which arises from his frequent use of the present tense; as Eaves and Kimpel indicate, the author consciously used this technique which he termed 'writing to the moment'.[29] Perhaps the most important feature of *Pamela* is its presentation of the heroine's feelings and her 'religious' reflections. As Dr Johnson commented, 'if you were to read Richardson for the story, your impatience would be so much fretted that you would hang yourself. *But you must read him for the sentiment, and consider the story as only giving occasion to the sentiment*'.[30] Given that the work is a novel of sentiment, its 'realism' is somewhat compromised. Much of that which Richardson presents as Pamela's thoughts and emotions amounts to little more than sermonising, but he does achieve a degree of psychological realism which was then innovative in the novel form. It is for this reason that the author could plausibly claim to have written according to nature whilst still pursuing a didactic purpose. In the second part of the novel Richardson appears to have run out of literary imagination, and it is even more blatantly didactic than the first part. In the absence of any major developments in Pamela's story the author fills his pages with tedious moralising and, on the most slender of pretexts, inserts a lot of irrelevant material such as a 39-page critique of Locke's *Some Thoughts Concerning Education*. As Tompkins maintains, Richardson saw his works as 'conduct-books' and furthermore, 'a little solid information, on whatever pretext inserted, was always favourably received – at least by the critics'.[31] However, such quantities of didactic matter inevitably undermine verisimilitude, and the immediacy of *Pamela* is noticeably lacking in the sequel.

Regarding the issue of individual-social integration mentioned in Chapter 1 of this study, Pamela can be seen as representing the moral individualism associated with the bourgeoisie; this, and her humble origins, places her outside of the class which Richardson considers appropriate for her. Throughout the novel B. – a member of the gentry – gradually comes to view Pamela as a worthy individual and ultimately appears to embrace the moral code, which she adheres to. Thus concessions on the part of the gentry and the subsequent incorporation of Pamela by marriage allow her upward mobility and decide the question of her social integration.

Turning to Sarah Fielding's *David Simple* we have to rely on the words of her brother, Henry, for an insight into the author's intentions: 'the Merit of this Work consists in a vast Penetration into human Nature, and a profound Discernment of all the Mazes, Windings and Labrinths, which perplex the Heart of Man to such a degree, that he is himself often incapable of seeing through them'.[32] This suggests that the work contains psychological investigation and understanding according to Kelsall, Richardson likewise believed that Sarah was 'a psychological novelist of the same kind as himself'.[33] However, as Kelsall recognises, this was not the case; the only real similarity between the two authors' works is that both are novels of sentiment in that they seek to draw an emotional response from the reader far more than to portray 'real life'. Sarah Fielding's characters are generally little more than formal types and are static and undeveloped – they do not have the reflexivity or immediacy of Pamela. So, when Henry Fielding goes on to state that Sarah's characters 'are as wonderfully drawn by the Writer, as they were by *Nature* herself', one can only assume that he was being generous in his assessment of his sister's work.[34] Unfortunately the inadequate portrayal of character, the fragmentary nature of the overall composition, and the overt didacticism of the work result in an ambling would-be-moralistic piece which fails to provide a coherent critique of the evils which Sarah Fielding wished to condemn. Perhaps, as Kelsall argues, she 'is not really a novelist at all', in any event, the book fares little better if one views it as a moral treatise for it leads the reader from one example of folly or wickedness to another, to no useful literary or philosophical purpose.[35]

Nevertheless, it is noteworthy that Henry Fielding claimed verisimilitude for the characters drawn by his sister, and likewise for the events in the novel: 'the Incidents arising from this Fable, tho' often surprizing, are everywhere natural, (Credibility not once being shocked through the whole)'.[36] In the sense that the text does not introduce dragons, miracles and the like, this is true. The high value placed upon a work being realistic is apparent from Henry Fielding's preface; similarly, Jane Collier who – it is thought – wrote the preface to Sarah's sequel, *Volume the Last*, writes therein of 'real Life (which these kind of Writings intend to represent)'.[37] She goes on to point out the particularity of the author's project when she states that: '*Her Intention is not to show how any Man, but how such a Man would support himself under the Worldly Misfortunes and Afflictions to which human-kind is liable*'.[38] This points up the idea that David is an exemplary character undergoing particular trials, and is not intended as a universal type.

Sarah Fielding's technique consists of employing an authorial overview to narrate the story of her hero, transporting him from one dire situation to another – she frequently speaks directly to the reader and comments upon the action as it unfolds. The composition is scrappy and anecdotal, a fault exacerbated by the inclusion of irrelevant, lengthy pieces such as the (54-page) story of Isabella. In both *David Simple* and *Volume The Last* one finds little development of plot or characters, the former being trivial and the latter wooden, David's singularity arises from his flawless character, boundless naivety, and tender feelings: in view of these traits he is usually considered to be one of the early heroes of sensibility. Fielding denies the possibility of David being integrated into society by placing him outside of the mainstream of social activity, in the company of a few similarly unworldly friends. However, even this escapist alternative to social integration is undermined by *Volume the Last* (published nine years after the original), in which David and most of his associates meet unhappy endings. Fielding's hero can neither be integrated into society, nor can he escape from it.

Henry Fielding clearly states the purpose behind *Amelia* in the dedication to his patron, Ralph Allen; he writes, 'The following book is sincerely designed to promote the cause of virtue, and to expose some of the most glaring evils, as well public as private, which at present infest this country'.[39] Here at the outset Fielding makes it apparent that his work has a moral purpose which goes beyond illustrating characters worthy of imitation: in fact he seeks to provide a limited critique of some institutionalised 'evils'. How far he succeeds is debatable, but there is no doubt that, in making the attempt, he helped to extend the scope of the novelist.

As Fielding explains in Chapter 1, some of the events surrounding Booth and Amelia are 'extraordinary' but, he insists, we can understand such events if we put aside notions of fortune and the like and seek to account for them by reference to 'natural means'.[40] In other words, according to Fielding, a careful examination of human life can reveal – in any particular case – the causal relationship between the contributory factors affecting that life. However, this is no purely philosophical enterprise: the point of the work resides in the fact that,

> 'as histories of this kind . . . may properly be called models of HUMAN LIFE, so, *by observing minutely the several incidents which tend to the catastrophe or completion of the whole, and the minute causes whence those incidents are produced, we shall best be instructed in this most useful of all arts, which I call the ART OF LIFE'.*[41]

Throughout the novel Fielding acts as omniscient narrator with little intrusion as the author; however, he does use Dr Harrison as a more-or-less direct channel for his own comments on a number of occasions and – without really building the character of a narrator – suggests that he (the narrator) is currently in contact with the heroine. This is done with devices such as 'Amelia declared to me the other day'.[42]

The focus on a married couple was unusual in itself, as Alter suggests:

> Fielding, as always, is highly conscious of his role as a pioneer: with the partial and uncomfortably didactic exception of the continuation of *Pamela*, no novel as yet had attempted to deal with what happens to two people *after* they unite in the state of matrimony, when, in place of the adventures or tensions of courtship, they must bear the heavy and multifarious responsibilities of making a life together.[43]

As Needham and Utter have observed, 'The typical plot of the English novel has love for the starting-post and marriage for the finish-line' so Fielding's originality here should not be overlooked.[44] Of course Fielding does not just concentrate upon the relation between individuals, but also tries to show their place in the wider society: thus he produced a work which does not have the narrow psychologically-oriented tension of *Pamela*, but which paints a more general picture of eighteenth-century institutions and social relations. The question of the individual and integration in the novel centres around Booth, an amiable but somewhat feckless character. The process of integration is complicated by the fact that Booth must not merely be integrated into the wider society (which is shown to be riddled with corruption and dishonesty), but rather within the ranks of those who pursue honest Christian lives against all the odds. To this end Booth is made to undergo an unconvincing conversion, Amelia's lost inheritance is retrieved (solving financial difficulties), and the couple retreat to the country away from the temptations and snares which surround them in the city.

In *The Spiritual Quixote*, Graves intially adopts the pose of editor in order to explain how the manuscript came to light: he may have done this simply for the fun of it, to conceal his authorship, or perhaps because such a long time (16 years) had passed between the writing of the piece and its publication that he thought it appropriate to present the novel as being of historical interest. I suspect that the first of these possibilities is the most likely. Nevertheless, when we move on to the fictitious author's preface, I think that we find a genuine statement of Graves's intent: 'The following narrative was intended to expose a species of folly, which has frequently disturbed the tranquillity of this nation'.[45] Graves sets out his objection to itinerancy and claims that his novel 'has a direct tendency to prevent Religion becoming ridiculous'.[46] Adopting the persona of editor again for the advertisement, Graves tells us that the supposed author was thought to be sympathetic to those he attacks in the text (the Methodists) – this has led some critics to ascribe such sympathy to Graves, as we shall see below.[47] After a dedication, a prefatory anecdote, the 'author's preface', a postscript, an advertisement, and another (joke) dedication, we come to the introduction wherein Graves states that he has tried to make the book interesting (likening it to the then popular travel tales). He goes on to claim, 'The reader will likewise meet with *several trifling incidents from real life*; which, however, the Author flatters himself, are so far disguised by an alteration of the circumstances of place and time, as to prevent a particular application – *unless where a particular application was intended*'.[48] This may be thought to be another of Graves's jokes, but as C. J. Hill has pointed out, there is much in the novel which is certainly drawn from Graves's own life – more of which later.

The Spiritual Quixote is loosely based on Cervantes's original, and aims to satirise eighteenth-century Methodist preachers; however, as Tracy has argued, Graves was somewhat influenced by Henry Fielding's notion of the 'comic epic in prose'.[49] The work is a variation on the picaresque theme, the main difference being that the hero is by no means a rogue. Graves employs authorial omniscience throughout and intrudes frequently to comment in detail upon certain aspects of the story. He also uses several characters to express his own religious views at length, and introduces a number of peripheral 'histories' such as that of Rivers and Charlotte.[50] This sort of material unnecessarily interrupts the sequence of events, and does not blend with the Smollett-like incident and humour at the heart of the novel. Graves's portrayal of the individual and society is based upon how his central character, Wildgoose, can be reintegrated into the gentry; the hero's initially imperfect integration being exacerbated by his decision to abandon everything in favour of itinerant preaching, a choice which entails downward mobility. However, his willingly adopted pariah status is overturned when he becomes reconciled to Anglicanism and marries a 'good' woman: he then takes up his rightful place in the community and resolves to leave spiritual and social questions to established authority.

In his advertisement for *The Vicar of Wakefield*, Goldsmith states that 'There are an hundred faults in this Thing, and an hundred things might be said to prove them beauties'.[51] The first part of the sentence is surely correct, but one may well have reservations regarding the rest of it. Goldsmith's apology implies that the most important question about the book is whether or not it is 'amusing', but he also seems to want to defend it on the grounds of its simplicity of content, and its presentation of religion. There has been a lot of debate concerning the form and content of this, Goldsmith's only novel, with some critics arguing that it displays ingenuity and the skilful use of irony, whilst others deem the work a shambles. Given the raggedness of the novel, its poor layout, and its change of tone after the first 16 chapters (in which it moves from comedy to what one writer has described as 'pathetic narrative' [52]), I am inclined to agree with those who think it badly written. Apart from the above reasons for viewing the novel as an artistic failure (it was initially a commercial failure too) which has been elevated by over-sophisticated modern interpretations, it is well known that Goldsmith was a vehement critic of novels generally, and therefore unlikely to produce a novel of his own for anything other than financial reasons. With the exception of those works which enjoyed enormous success during the eighteenth century, the novel was considered to be a very easy form for writers and therefore did not usually command much respect. Wardle states that Goldsmith, replying to a friend's suggestions as to how his novel could be improved, said that 'it was not worth the effort, since he would not be paid for his pains'.[53] Regarding novels more generally, Sells claims that Goldsmith 'set little store by the novel and none at all by the novels which were published in his own day. He thought nothing of Fielding'.[54] According to Lytton Sells, Goldsmith also disliked Smollett (at least, prior to Smollett employing him) and Sterne, and made his dislike so well known that 'he actually became involved in a brawl' as a consequence of this. Perhaps most interesting of all is the fact that 'In January 1759 he had advised his brother not to allow the latter's son to read romances or novels, since they depict a happiness which has never existed'.[55] In my opinion this is most ironic, for as Allen maintains, 'Goldsmith of all writers was the least cut out to be a realistic novelist, and what he achieved was something very different from what he intended; instead of the near-tragedy of a man who brought himself and his family to ruin he produced something very much like a fairy tale, an idealised picture of rural life, with a delightful Quixotic comic character at the centre and with Burchell as an awkward eighteenth-century good fairy to contrive a happy ending'.[56] If Allen is right in thinking that Goldsmith's intention was to write a realistic novel, one wonders how the author viewed *The Vicar of Wakefield* when he had completed it: within a few years of having attacked novels for portraying an unreal happiness, he had penned one which included all of those features which he supposedly despised.

The story of Dr Primrose and his family is told by the former, in the first person – thus the narrator is also the main character of the piece. Both the Vicar and Burchell, the two 'good' men in the story, speak for Goldsmith in a number of places and thus his Tory-Anglican views are scattered throughout. As Friedman has observed, '*The Vicar of Wakefield* is extraordinarily digressive even for a novel written in an age very tolerant of digressions in fiction'.[57] These constant interruptions in the narrative suggest that the author took little care and/or had little skill in manipulating the form which he derided; furthermore, of all of the novels considered in this study, *The Vicar of Wakefield* is probably the most crudely ideological.

The hero, Primrose, is – in spite of his eccentric personal and religious views – integrated within his community when the novel opens, but this integration is disrupted when the family are forced to move to another parish and accept a humbler way of life. The Vicar's wife and daughters are never really reconciled to this change, and

Olivia, the eldest daughter, later becomes further isolated as a result of her 'fall'. Her integration is only achieved when it is disclosed that she was legally married to the man who sought to seduce her, whilst the rest of the family – including the Vicar – are reabsorbed, and even socially enhanced by the marriage of their youngest daughter, Sophia, to the aristocrat, Burchell.

Fanny Burney, in her preface to *Evelina*, begins by stating that novelists are the least respected of all writers but goes on to list Rousseau, Johnson, Marivaux, Fielding and Richardson as having saved the form from contempt. In view of their achievements, she argues, there is nothing shameful in attempting 'this species of writing'. Having made this apology Burney then goes on to outline her project; 'To draw characters from nature though not from life, and to mark the manners of the times, is the attempted plan of the following letters'.[58] In this way Burney commits herself to the realistic presentation of characters and their various milieux and, having argued that the popularity of novels (particularly amongst young women) was unlikely to decline in the near future, she proceeds to propose that those works which are not injurious should be encouraged. The author herself completely eschews 'the fantastic regions of romance, where fiction is coloured by all the gay tints of luxurious imagination, where reason is an outcast, and where the sublimity of the marvellous rejects aid from all sober probability'. Her heroine is, maintains Burney, 'the offspring of nature', and not some implausible 'faultless monster'.[59]

Burney then discusses the importance of originality in novel-writing, concluding that 'In books . . . imitation cannot he shunned too sedulously'; however, she recognises that it is difficult to avoid the commonplace without having recourse to 'unnatural' subjects. Whilst playing down her own claim to originality, Burney contends that the aforementioned writers whom she cites as influences – have 'culled the flowers' from the paths which they chose to explore, thus forcing her to choose a different direction.[60]

Evelina is an epistolary novel told mainly through the character of Evelina herself – thus events and characters appear to the reader via the subjectivity of an adolescent girl making her 'entrance into the world'.[61] Perhaps the most important character apart from the heroine is Villars, her guardian, whose letters to Lady Howard and Evelina serve to move the story along and to provide a contrast to the world of fashion and rank in which Burney places her nervous young heroine. Villars is the main vehicle for didacticism in the work, his frequent advice amounting to a fairly full conduct-guide. The characters in *Evelina* are mostly well sketched, and often very amusing, and there is less discrepancy between major and minor protagonists than one finds in a great many other eighteenth-century novels. However, there is no sustained attempt to examine the subjectivity of anyone other than the heroine, and consequently the other characters sometimes appear dull or flimsy compared to Evelina. Nevertheless, the novel was very successful and, as Spacks has noted, 'It has been admired ever since its own time for the accuracy of its social detail and conversation'.[62] Allen, who thinks Burney overrated, himself remarks upon her 'camera-eye' and 'microphone-ear', so it would seem that the author's skill in this respect has been recognised by both her contemporaries and her subsequent critics.[63] As Spacks contends in her discussion of Burney's journals and novels, and their relation to the author's own life, *Evelina* 'manifests a high level of psychological insight closely related to the self-knowledge that emerges from even the youthful diaries'.[64] This insight resides in Burney's understanding of female anxieties and conflicts, maintains Spacks, illustrating Fanny Burney's own personality with the following quotation: 'The fear of doing wrong has always been the leading principle of my internal guidance'.[65] These words would fit easily into her heroine's mouth.

Evelina has been denied her rightful status; this and her rural upbringing make her something of an outsider in the aristocratic company in which she finds herself. However, Burney ensures Evelina's complete integration when the girl is accepted by her noble father, Sir John Belmont, and finally married to Lord Orville.

Robert Bage's *Hermsprong* contains no dedication, preface, or introduction expressing the writer's intention, however, the sub-title of the piece indicates that Bage sought to create an ideal rather than a realistic hero: 'Man as He is Not'. Scott thought that Bage was generally concerned with the presentation of character rather than narrative, and Tompkins suggests that *Hermsprong* departs from Bage's previous novels: 'Hitherto he has been evolving a novel of manners and character, stripped of improbable turns of fortune and strengthened by a strong speculative interest. Now, forsaking the natural fluidity of this form, he writes a book in which the tendentious elements have stiffened into a bizarre framework'.[66] As Tompkins further argues, in *Hermsprong* the author's manipulation of his characters is obvious and therefore 'They are ingredients in a pattern rather than individuals, and they are stripped of all complexities of character in order that the pattern may not be disturbed'.[67] The fact that the characters are – with the possible exception of Miss Fluart – so poorly developed and the plot so thin may well explain why critics like Allen insist upon labelling Bage 'A doctrinaire novelist proper'. However, whilst it is undeniable that Bage wrote with his political views to the fore, the woodenness of *Hermsprong* is the result of something other than Bage's politics.[68] The simplistic plot and lack of attention to character conspire to make the novel static and uninspired; Hermsprong's speeches certainly do not help the work, it is true, but equally damaging are Bage's frequent attempts at wit, which by and large fail miserably.

Wilkins has noted that in *Hermsprong*, Bage 'displays the contemporary scene through the agency of a critical witness from another sphere': this technique was quite common in eighteenth-century English novels, and all that need be said here is that what Bage actually does with his hero is to put forward a very limited bourgeois critique of the aristocracy, some Anglican ministers, and contemporary attitudes towards women.

The story is related by Gregory Glen, himself a character in the action which takes place; after explaining how he came to be involved, Glen ceases to speak in the first person and adopts the position of omniscient narrator. Prior to this he informs us that he does not write for fame, fortune, or to instruct – unfortunately he never does state his intentions. Bage, in this guise, refers to critics and readers in a number of places and makes no effort to sustain a continuous artistic illusion throughout the novel.[69] Whatever the rights or wrongs of this, it also detracts from the work, and all of Bage's feeble efforts to be humorous do not repair the damage. Hermsprong is, of course, what Allen terms an 'ideal creation': he was intended as such and Bage did not seek to convince readers that he was anything else.[70]

Hermsprong differs from the other central characters discussed so far in that he is initially shown as a complete outsider, and critic of the environment in which he appears. As the representative of moral and intellectual ideas alien to those who surround him, it seems that Hermsprong is both unwilling and unable to be integrated into the community. However, Bage ultimately retreats from this position, implying that the hero's views are reconcilable with the very institutions which he has previously attacked. Thus integration is fostered by trivialising the conflicting ideologies and practices shown in the first part of the novel into a conflict between good and bad individuals. Additionally, the revelation that Hermsprong has noble blood allows automatic integration into the socio-political hierarchy which he has seemingly opposed until the near-conclusion of the novel.

We can briefly summarise our writers' didactic purposes in relation to ideology. Richardson's *Pamela* is unashamedly didactic and sought to provide moral guidance (particularly for young women) in a wholly serious manner. His support for individualism was, however, uneven; he accepted the view that individuals should be assessed according to their own merits or failings, rather than their class position, just as he considered the individual to be the primary unit in matters of religion and conscience. However, he did not advocate social change in order to encourage individualism in any sphere, and his general attitude towards social organisation suggests that he thought it best left alone. Richardson made it clear that he did not wish to give servants and others ideas inappropriate to their station, but rather promoted the belief that exceptional persons would inevitably be rewarded, in heaven if not on earth. He took social integration for granted, whilst assuming that those with particular merits might well become upwardly mobile and thus integrated into a higher level of the hierarchy than that from which they had originated. Ideologically, Richardson's message urged people to be content with their lot and to rest safe in the knowledge that they would get their just deserts; he certainly did not recommend that individuals should actively strive to improve their own social, political, or economic standing. The author who has so frequently been deemed the archetypal bourgeois novelist of the eighteenth-century actually showed extensive support for the status quo: Richardson 'represented' the bourgeoisie in a period when most of them accepted their servile status *vis-à-vis* the ruling class almost without question.

Like Richardson, Sarah Fielding supported *moral* individualism; she did not favour the values associated with economic individualism. Her didacticism – similarly lacking in humour – ignored the possibility of social change, arguing that a better society was dependent upon a change in individuals. In the absence of such change she saw no way in which altruistic and honest persons could be integrated into the self-interested and corrupt society which she portrayed in *David Simple*. Social mobility plays little part in the novel, and the essence of Sarah Fielding's ideological pronouncements is that everyone should be altruistic and content: the only goals which she saw as legitimate for the individual were those such as the.pursuit of 'purity' in heart and mind.

In contrast Henry Fielding's didacticism in *Amelia* involves some attempt to criticise existing institutions and practices. Whilst avoiding the melancholy atmosphere of *David Simple*, Fielding indicated his distaste for the individualistic society in which he set *Amelia*. He implies that individualism – along with corruption and dishonesty – are characteristic of city life, and that Christians cannot be comfortably integrated into such milieux. Only in the comparatively untainted rural areas, suggests Fielding, can any genuine and worthwhile individual–social integration be achieved. Although Fielding shares the belief that individuals must have a change of heart for any extensive social change to occur, he also advocates legal reform as a means of tackling both institutional and personal corruption for, he maintains, decent people can only thrive in a just and well-regulated society based upon Christian precepts.

Graves's didactic task in *The Spiritual Quixote* is that of exposure and criticism, achieved with the weapon of satire. However, whereas Fielding had misgivings about established institutions and authority, Graves stoutly defends them and levels his charges against (in particular) critics of, and rivals to, the Anglican Church. Graves was no exponent of individualism, and the small measure of support which it received from him rested largely on his belief that individuals should mind their own affairs. He assumed that individuals would be integrated into their own local communities but that within such communities, and indeed in the wider society, they should concentrate upon their own direct personal concerns. Graves saw no need whatsoever for social change, although if he had done so there is no doubt that he would have considered innovation to be the prerogative of established religious and secular authority. Graves did intimate that he thought upward mobility was sometimes justifiable, but his main concern regarding social mobility in the novel involves ridiculing religious enthusiasts for their apparent readiness to 'lower' themselves. His ideological position amounted to unequivocal support for the status quo.

Goldsmith was similarly resistant to most forms of social change, especially in relation to the Church and the monarchy. His didacticism operates via the lengthy political speeches of his central characters, wherein the middle class are supported, but change (with the exception of certain legal reforms) is eschewed. Goldsmith took the integration of the individual more or less for granted but, judging by

The Vicar of Wakefield, thought upward mobility an acceptable goal. The essence of Goldsmith's ideology is that traditional authority should be wholeheartedly supported and that all – including the poor – should be reconciled to existing conditions. To promote this view he sought to deny that the rich had any advantages over the exploited, arguing that the latter were fully compensated in 'heaven'.

Fanny Burney's *Evelina* has a somewhat narrower focus than the other works, and is only really didactic in the sense that it can be seen a conduct-guide for young women: one which is rather uncritical of the position of women generally. The background assumptions of the novel are individualistic, and it does not seem to occur to Burney that the social order can or should be modified. She assumed that individuals would be integrated into the appropriate rank, and took a fairly severe view of those whom she portrayed as actively seeking social advancement. Her main ideological claim appears to be that propriety, obedience, and deference in women are desirable (and rewarded), and the that the modest and 'pure-hearted' triumph where self-seekers fail.

Robert Bage, on the other hand, airs a good many socio-political opinions in *Hermsprong*, often in a somewhat contradictory manner. Bage was very much influenced by the basic tenets of individualism, and his central character epitomises what he took to be the best qualities of 'individualistic' man. In some sections of the novel Bage seems to be arguing for radical social change, but he eventually retreats and allows his ideal individual to become part of the establishment. Ideologically, Bage appears to have thought that individualism represented the highest goal for human beings, and that it is only in terms of individuals that any aspect of social organisation can be assessed. This individualism is not, however, a licence to challenge the Church and the monarchy: how far Bage's attitude was dictated by expediency here remains debatable. Nevertheless, as the novel stands the only message it conveys is that 'bad' individuals should be excluded from power and that a more egalitarian attitude should be shown towards people in general, and women in particular.

Having made these preliminary comments, we can now consider the seven novels in greater detail, starting with the most famous and controversial of them, Samuel Richardson's *Pamela*.

Part Two

3

Samuel Richardson:
Pamela (1740)

Pamela is the story of a servant girl who successfully resists the sexual advances of her young master until he marries her: thus she transcends the problem of being 'poor but honest' via her upward mobility into the gentry.

Several themes related to the social hierarchy and relations of the period occur throughout the novel, not least the idea that poverty and honesty are always preferable to riches and dishonesty. For Pamela this is axiomatic, so when B. threatens to discharge her for disobeying him she is convinced that a return to poverty will cause her far less distress than the moral and sexual surrender which he demands.[1] Indeed she feels so strongly about her honesty or virtue – terms used to signify, primarily, sexual virginity – that she later claims: 'I would marry a man who begs from door to door, and has no home, rather than endanger my honesty'.[2] Consequently B.'s attempts to lure Pamela with fine clothes and jewellery are doomed to failure.[3]

As the novel progresses and it becomes apparent that Pamela will not have to choose between honesty and affluence, her statements begin to imply that poverty is not merely a trial which can be endured but is perhaps enjoyable and admirable in itself.[4] When Pamela's father suggests that he and his wife will disgrace their daughter in view of their poverty and her forthcoming marriage, she tells him, 'Your poverty has been my glory and my riches'.[5] However, if poverty is here shown to be bearable and even accompanied by certain advantages, riches are presented as a heavy burden – as Pamela outlines in verse

> For, Oh we pity should the great,
> Instead of envying their estate;
> Temptations always on 'em wait,
> Exempt from which are such as we.

> Their riches, gay deceitful snares,
> Enlarge their fears, increase their cares;
> Their servants' joy surpasses theirs;
> At least, so judges Pamela.[6]

According to this view, wealth involves so many problems that one cannot understand why people seek to gain and maintain it. However, Pamela herself knows that the rich are more powerful than the poor, as becomes apparent when she states: 'power and riches never want advocates' and, to B., 'if you were not rich and great, and I poor and little, you would not insult me thus'.[7] So when Pamela rhetorically asks, 'what can the abject poor do against the mighty rich, when they are determined to oppress?', we know – as did Richardson – that the consensus would be 'very little'.[8] Nevertheless whilst 'power and riches never want to promote their vilest ends', the poor have fewer opportunities to break moral laws and this – Richardson's view as expressed by Pamela – implies that the poor may frequently be morally superior to their wealthy counterparts. This suggests to me the formal nature of the morality lauded in *Pamela*.

In spite of the fact that Pamela claims that happiness is possible in 'beloved poverty' her remarks on the condition are later qualified. Although having stated that she would rather marry a beggar than even risk her honesty, she is clearly upset when Lady Davers labels her 'beggar-born' and a 'beggarly brat'. This charges Pamela's parents with extreme poverty, and she replies: 'Good Madam . . . spare my dear parents. They are honest and industrious; they were once in a very creditable way, and never were beggars'.[9] Being part of the 'honest and industrious' poor, hard-working and deferential, sets one above the lowest ranks of society. As far as the ruling class were concerned the salient fact about people like Pamela's parents was that, in Walzer's words, 'the poverty of the "industrious poor" . . . led neither to disorder nor discontent'.[10] It is this section of the community that Pamela intends to help once married to B., her enthusiasm for philanthropy depending at least in part upon her expectation of the prayers and blessings of the poor for her husband.[11] This is a rather surprising attitude towards charity coming from a post-Puritan Anglican, but the balance is evened up as we learn that Pamela is only concerned with local, worthy paupers, and that she intends to help them according to a rational system of administration (including an account book in which she has written '*Humble returns for Divine Mercies*').[12] She claims no credit for such charity, supposing herself to be an instrument of Providence.

Apart from her comments upon the fact that the rich can pursue their interests even when these are morally wrong, Pamela makes few serious criticisms of her socio-economic superiors. She thinks that B. is both spoilt and easily angered, but sees this as a misfortune of his sex and class. When she reads Lady Davers's negative opinion of B.'s intention to marry a social inferior she does, however, criticise the pride of the rich and the disdain they have for the humble: 'O keep me, heaven, from *their* high condition, if my mind shall ever be tainted with *their* vice, or polluted with so cruel and inconsiderate a contempt of that humble estate they behold with so much scorn!'[13] Nevertheless Pamela tends to pity rather than criticise the wealthy and, whilst she believes that they should use some of their resources charitably, she does not see anything amiss in the existence of enormous financial inequality – something she supposes to be divinely ordained:

Wise Providence
Does various parts for various minds dispense:
The *meanest slaves,* or those whose *hedge* and *ditch,*
Are useful, by their sweat, to feed the *rich.*
The *rich,* in due return, impart their store,
Which comfortably feeds the lab'ring *poor.*
 Nor let the *rich* the *lowest slave* disdain:
He's *equally* a *link* of Nature's *chain;*
Labours to the *same end,* joins in *one view;*
And *both alike* the Will Divine pursue;
And, at the last, are levell'd, *king and slave*
Without distinction, in the silent grave.[14]

The above verse constitutes a compressed account of Pamela's understanding of social relations.

Pamela is not merely complacent about social relations, however; in Richardson's continuation she goes so far as to state: 'it is my absolute opinion, that degrees in general should be kept up'.[15] No doubt the author put these words into her mouth to deflect the charge made by some of his contemporaries that he opposed social inequality – a number of commentators had seized upon what they took to be a 'levelling' tendency in *Pamela* Part One. In fact it is clear from Pamela's many conversations with B. in the original novel that she is a defender of the status quo and a nice critic of those who do not act in accordance with their social position. From B.'s first advances, Pamela chides him for ignoring the 'distance' between them and thus 'demeaning' himself; throughout the story she seems to be preoccupied with the fear that B. risks 'disgracing' himself amongst his peers and in front of his servants.[16] Moreover although Pamela frequently reiterates her own low status she solemnly offers B. advice as to how he should behave – and this is social, not moral, advice: 'I think you ought to regard the world's opinion, and avoid doing any thing disgraceful to your birth and fortune; . . . a little time, absence, and the conversation of worthier persons of my sex, will effectually enable you to overcome a regard so unworthy of your condition'. She concludes: 'I shall wish you happy in a lady of suitable degree'.[17]

Yet in spite of Pamela's constant references to her own low station and her unworthiness regarding B., this is not because she sees herself as nothing more than a common servant. She is particularly anxious to protect B. by hiding the real nature of his behaviour towards her from the other servants – this in itself indicates that she sees herself as being somewhat above her peers. She is certainly not, as Eagleton has suggested, an 'inconspicuous serving maid'; Pamela has enjoyed a privileged position in service and with the encouragement of her former mistress has further distanced herself from her fellow servants by acquiring skills in singing and dancing – accomplishments usually reserved for the daughters of the wealthy. Most importantly, as Watt et al. have pointed out, Pamela's concern for her chastity makes her atypical – more of which later.[18]

Whilst Pamela plays the humble servant, her general attitude towards her peers is what one might expect from an overseer, that is, she considers her master's interests over and above those of the other servants. Although it is Pamela's pleas which persuade B. to reinstate the servants whom he has unjustly dismissed, and whilst she does show some generosity to these former colleagues once she is married, her actions here proceed from Christian charity rather than any identification or solidarity with the servants.[19] In short, Pamela, with her exceedingly deferential stance towards the gentry, has few qualms about moving up the socio-economic scale away from the servants, however much she implies that she must distance herself from them simply to preserve B.'s dignity.[20]

B. does act in a manner likely to engender criticism from his own class when he marries his late mother's maidservant, but for all the talk 'demeaning' in the early part of the novel he does nothing remarkable prior to this. The contemporary sexual double-standard was such that no man in B.'s position would be thought

to be demeaning himself simply because he tried to seduce a socially-inferior girl. Such activities were not only largely taken for
granted, but were also considered trivial and unimportant in relation to any high-status seducer's rank or dignity. As Spacks has
indicated, B. sees his initial attempts to seduce Pamela 'as belonging
to a pattern so familiar as to be virtually devoid of meaning'.[21] B. has
nothing to lose in terms of honour or respect (discounting personal
pride) *until he decides to marry Pamela*; up to that point he has acted,
as Pamela herself observes, like most of the other gentlemen in the
local community and differs from them only in so far as he has
become so besotted by a socially-inferior woman that he will go to
extraordinary lengths to secure her.[22] For Richardson, B.'s stance
denotes 'love', but for countless critics – both in Richardson's
time and since – it looks like lust, obsession, lack of self-control and
so on.[23]

Even when B. has determined to marry Pamela they both remain
apprehensive about the likely response from members of B.'s class;
as Spacks remarks, 'Mr.B. and his bride share from the beginning
their assumption that the judgement of "the world" matters enor-
mously'.[24] In the event it is only Lady Davers (B.'s sister) who really
takes them to task and it is not long before she is won over.[25] B. then
proclaims to Pamela his reasons for having chosen her as a spouse –
in essence his choice seems to have been based upon her remarkable
deference more than her exemplary virtue. Sketching his requirements in a wife – which are considerable – B. frankly admits that he
would be unlikely to get the degree of respect and obedience which
he demands from a social equal. And B. here makes it plain that
whilst he appreciates Pamela's beauty and character, above all else
he expects her to obey him and maintain her characteristic subservience. *Pace* K. Rogers, Richardson did not think that marriage was a
'partnership between equals' – as we shall see.[26] Pamela, – ever-
willing to obey – codifies B.'s pronouncements into forty-eight 'rules'
or propositions to be studied and adhered to.[27]

Konigsberg, discussing the 'poor, virtuous girl weds rich man'
theme common to *Pamela* and other tales, suggests that it 'pleases the
lower class by giving hope for social advancement, and satisfies the
higher class by fostering equilibrium in society and giving expression to its males' desires to possess women more earthy than women
of their own class.[28] The point about offering hope to a lower class in
this way, and the view that cross-class marriages could play some
part in maintaining social stability are, I think, relevant. The theme

of female upward mobility via marriage was certainly well known and often used in eighteenth-century English novels. However, whilst women thus became (in fact and fiction) a focal point of class compromise, one may doubt that the 'earthiness' of lower-class women played much part in the process. No man of B.'s class would have had the slightest difficulty in possessing more poor women than he could possibly have coped with, and such a man would hardly have resorted to reading stories like *Pamela* in order to gratify any desire for a socially-inferior woman. Moreover, as Stone has indicated, there is some evidence to suggest that when members of 'the quality' took mistresses in eighteenth-century England, the women were usually 'from a well-to-do professional or merchant background'; thus they differed little from the wives of the men who kept them.[29] Throughout the eighteenth century, marriages between members of the gentry and women of the bourgeoisie became increasingly common, but such matches usually depended upon financial and political considerations more than anything else. Where straightforward personal choice was involved it seems likely that physical beauty and deference would most attract a man to a socially-inferior woman.

Modern commentators on Richardson often portray him as a 'Puritan' and suggest that *Pamela* displays such an outlook; Eagleton goes so far as to refer to the author as a 'puritan ideologue'.[30] Yet whilst there is some evidence of Puritan influence, it is wrong to suppose that Richardson's attitudes, as expressed in *Pamela*, can be quite so easily and unequivocally placed. Richardson, like many of his contemporaries held some opinions which might ultimately be traced to Puritanism, but there was a considerable distance between his beliefs and those held by the Puritans of the preceding two centuries. In modified form many ideas which were once thought peculiar to Puritanism had, by the mid-eighteenth century, become the common property of British culture; it was in this sense that Puritanism – although defeated politically in the seventeenth century – continued to live in subsequent ages. Therefore, to argue that Richardson was particularly representative of Puritan thinking is very misleading; if a candidate had to be found amongst eighteenth-century English prose writers then Defoe might more justifiably be considered. There is no evidence to suggest that Richardson's contemporaries saw him in this light, and it is hard to imagine why his critics should have failed to employ the unflattering term 'Puritan' to him and his work had they thought it to be remotely applicable.[31]

Like the Puritans, Richardson thought that marriage was a blessed state and that individuals should be allowed to choose their own spouse. However, Puritans believed that partners should be chosen according to their moral worth or 'godliness', and it is obvious that B. would not fulfil this requirement.[32] Moreover, as noted above, we have seen that practical rather than spiritual considerations influenced B.'s choice of Pamela for a wife. Within marriage, both Richardson and the Puritans assumed that the husband would be the dominant partner (a view peculiar to neither as it was traditional throughout European society); for the latter this assumption was based upon the idea that a husband would be morally superior to his wife but, as is reiterated throughout *Pamela*, Richardson's heroine is unquestionably of a higher moral status than her husband. In spite of this the author lets his heroine describe B. as 'the kind protector of my weakness, and the guide and director of my future steps'.[33] Walzer has argued that 'Puritan writers insisted upon the inferiority of the female, but nevertheless recognised in her the potential saint'; Richardson followed them in that much but departed from them by blithely subjecting his heroine to a man like B.[34] For Richardson, B.'s high rank is ample compensation for his low moral status; had Pamela been a Puritan she would have left B.'s household, regardless of the material consequences, at the first sign of any improper advance towards her. In so doing she would have obeyed the express wishes of her parents.[35]

Puritan attitudes towards parental authority were somewhat equivocal; notwithstanding the patriarchal management of the 'little commonwealth' advocated by Puritan preachers, the individualism inherent in the Puritan conception of the relation between each human being and God, and the emphasis upon each person's right to seek grace regardless of family ties, ultimately tended to minimise passive acceptance of parental control. In Pamela's case there could have been no question of her justifiably ignoring her parents' advice, Puritan or not; as Ball remarks, 'While it cannot be claimed that Pamela directly disobeys her parents in this instance, it cannot be claimed that she gives them the consideration that a morally respectable child should'.[36] But Pamela acts independently of her parents throughout the novel, for all her talk of being dutiful; in Richardson's continuation we find that *she gives her father advice rather than vice versa*, thus implying that social status determines wisdom beyond age. At various points in the story Pamela states that she is virtuous because of her upbringing – that is, because of the good example and religious teaching of her parents and her late mistress; B. claims that his own faults arise from the fact that he was not controlled or restrained as a child.[37] Whilst Pamela mentions God's grace in this context, the emphasis in her pronouncements is upon socialisation rather than grace itself; in this I think that Richardson departs from Puritanism. He continually stresses the importance of example in *Pamela*, whereas Puritans – broadly following Calvinist teaching – tended to concentrate more upon grace than anything else which might influence the individual's spiritual being.[38] However, this is a question of emphasis rather than one of fundamental disagreement; as we are told that Pamela's two (dead) brothers have been instrumental in bringing the family into poverty, the implication is that parental example alone cannot ensure that the child becomes a worthy adult.[39]

As much of *Pamela* takes the form of a personal journal, this may seem to indicate that the heroine monitors her thoughts and actions in a manner similar to that displayed in Puritan diaries and spiritual autobiographies.[40] However, unlike Pamela's journal, those written by Puritans recorded spiritual progress in detail, and were not simply a narrative of worldly events in one's life with some 'religious' reflections scattered throughout. Puritan diaries were basically confessional and meditative, and typically came to light posthumously; in contrast, Pamela's journal is addressed to her parents and is eventually read by, or to, her husband and his friends and relatives.[41] Pamela, then, writes for a secular audience. Such a character would be unlikely to produce a spiritual journal, not least because she has no enduring sense of sin, and is continually proclaiming her honesty and innocence; as Mrs Jervis says of her, 'I never found her inclinable to think herself in a fault'.[42] Whereas Puritan journals dwelt upon consciousness of sin and the struggles and temptations leading to progress or setbacks which formed the basis of spiritual reflection, Pamela's journal consists mainly of her hopes and fears regarding *secular* events. The heroine's only temptation involves her brief consideration of suicide (and her motives for pondering this course of action, to escape violation and exercise revenge, are noteworthy); she can hardly be said to have been engaged in the kind of spiritual battle described by Puritans. Pamela does not grow spiritually through the course of the novel; as the story is predicated upon her near-complete virtue she can have no conversion or rebirth. Consequently her letters and journal merely chart her secular progress: her upward mobility. Spacks has pointed out that 'To remain essentially the same, in many eighteenth-century novels, constitutes the central character's triumph', and Pamela appears to be an example of this proposition.[43] Likewise, B. undergoes no spiritual transformation but supposedly reforms; both the manner and quality of his development suggest formal repentance and an eye for practical considerations, and have little in common with the Puritan experience.

More generally Pamela's acceptance and defence of the social hierarchy does not accord with Puritanism. The extent to which Puritans felt able to tolerate this hierarchy (which included the monarchy and the episcopacy) varied somewhat, but none would have held the traditional and subservient attitude towards rank displayed by Pamela; they did not suppose social relations to be divinely ordained, as she does. The fact that she continues to respect B. after he has attempted to seduce her on several occasions itself shows a non-Puritan deference to social rather than moral stature; additionally Puritans did not support the double-standard relating to sexual conduct which Richardson, by failing to punish B. and even allowing him to wed the heroine, here shows himself to be complacent about.[44] Just as Pamela's 'virtue' was, for Richardson, her most important characteristic, so B.'s high social position is shown to be more significant than his lechery. Pamela forgives this all too easily if we mistakenly suppose that she accurately represents Puritanism.

Although neither the Established Church nor its ministers play much part in *Pamela*, Richardson viewed the Church as both legitimate and essentially sound; when not indisposed by his various ailments the author himself attended Anglican services. In the novel there is one good Anglican minister, Williams, and one dubious one, Peters, but Richardson nowhere suggests that there is any need for Church reform. And he can only advise clergymen beset by 'proud patrons' to be pious and trust to Providence.[45] However the issue of Church reform was the most important single factor uniting the Puritans of the previous two centuries. Whether Presbyterians or Independents, the Puritans fought against Episcopacy; Richardson did not. The overall impression created by *Pamela* is that Richardson did not have much interest in religious issues, but rather saw religion as, on the one hand, a useful means of maintaining the existing social order, whilst on the other, it could help to promote refinement in the area of manners. Richardson's determination to positively sanction Pamela's conduct with the secular rewards of upward mobility, wealth and fulsome praise, itself indicates a prudential approach towards morality. Virtue, as many of Richardson's critics have argued, is supposed to be its own reward – something which the author was loath to accept.[46] I conclude that the calculating and self-righteous atmosphere which pervades *Pamela* was in marked contrast to the practical vigour and spiritual seriousness generated by radical-Protestantism, and epitomised by Puritanism.

Perhaps the most significant feature of *Pamela* is that it presents us with an ideal which Richardson thought appropriate for women; the model is offered for the imitation of all women regardless of class. The author thought that there was one correct line of conduct for women, and he tried to universalise a set of 'feminine' qualities which he saw as both fitting and uplifting for the 'dear' sex. Pamela is a representative of Richardson's views regarding women, and she illustrates the kind of characteristics which he deemed thoroughly admirable.

Watt has argued that 'the legal position of women in the eighteenth century was very largely governed by the patriarchal concepts of Roman law', and has further observed that, 'the patriarchal legal situation of married women made it impossible for them to realize the aims of economic individualism'.[47] He goes on to cite the example of Defoe's Roxana as a successful, unmarried businesswoman, but accepts that autonomous economic action/independence was a difficult goal for women – married or single – to achieve. Even the unmarried Roxana's economic successes were not only atypical, but were also based upon, and inseparable from, her recurring violations of moral law. These transgressions eventually lead her to be complicit in the breaking of juridical law and the Biblical commandment, 'Thou shalt not kill'. And this, as Roxana herself concludes, heralds her final downfall. Watt further suggests that 'the conception of sex we find in Richardson embodies a more complete and comprehensive separation between the male and female roles than had previously existed', but does not relate this to his own points about patriarchy noted above.[48] I would argue that it is the anomalous position of women – subject to patriarchal control – in an increasingly individualist society which helps to foster the creation of a complex, specifically feminine code of conduct. Such a code would serve to explain and justify the situation of the many women who, as a result of economic developments, were increasingly excluded from what came to be considered the most important sphere of individual action and achievement: the economy. If men were to make their mark by their prowess in this expanding area (whether from adherence to the older accumulative propositions associated with Calvinism or in accordance with the secular aim of wealth for power and luxury), women were recruited in growing numbers to the contracting realm of religion and morality. Though never to achieve the highest command in this domain, women were good enough to act as enthusiastic supporters and defenders of the new faith of chastity, propriety, prudence and delicacy. This dogma, largely produced by men for the observance of women did, however, offer the individual woman the opportunity to became a heroine. It is as if the forces of the bourgeoisie during this period divided along sex lines: the men to wage war on the economic front, that is to act practically whilst the women – defenders of form rather than content – were left to struggle in the realm of the ideal, supported by ideologists drawn from both sexes. Of course this does over-simplify things and implies a lack of interconnection between practical and ideal interests which cannot withstand close scrutiny; nevertheless it is this impression which strikes one when pondering the channelling of male and female energy into superficially separate projects.

These activities were actually complementary and, if women consequently played a smaller part in the economy, they were to be rewarded with increased leisure, entertainment and socio-moral status. The sphere of morality constituted their very own means of ascension, and the female champion of manners and morality was ensured respect and accorded honour by both the men and the women of the middle class – even if she did not have the good fortune to climb the social hierarchy as deftly as Pamela. Such were the rewards for female heroism and such was the circumscribed campaign in which heroically – inclined women were encouraged to excel.[49] They did not even have to leave the house. Caution was required, however, for to stray onto the wrong battlefield – to the terrain contested by men – was to abandon all pretensions to heroism, or even to simple modesty.

This ideology, which Richardson and his contemporaries played such a major part in creating, was not merely one of obedience and respect rewarded. However much it *may* have contributed to a somewhat more respectful attitude towards women on the part of men, there can be little doubt that – in providing women with a potential domain of excellence – it also involved judging female conduct with reference to an expanding range of exacting standards. If the 'angels' of the middle class derived some benefits from this new mode of exaltation, they likewise now had further to fall if they failed to satisfy their rigorous examiners. The point becomes relevant when we consider the following: Watt has claimed that there is a 'decarnalization of the public feminine role' in eighteenth-century England, and has suggested that Richardson and his allies played an important part in this process.[50] The author's stance, continues Watt, promoted the idea that women are immune from 'sexual feelings' and that they marry 'because the pieties of marriage and the family were safe only in their hands'.[51] Such a view was, maintains, Watt, who himself tends to stress the influence of Puritanism in Richardson's work, 'directly opposed to the earlier attitudes of Puritanism itself, where figures such as Calvin, John Knox, and Milton were notoriously prone to lay more emphasis on the concupiscence of women than of men'. This puzzles Watt, who muses, 'Exactly why the serpent's invidious connection with Eve should have been forgotten is not clear'.[52]

The answer to this apparent paradox (quite apart from the fact that, as I have argued above, Richardson was not especially representative of Puritanism) is that Richardson had by no means forgotten about the 'invidious connection'. For all of the author's supposed devotion to women and their advancement, he did not think that they were morally reliable to the extent that they could be allowed to have control over their own lives; as the Puritans whom Watt cites were convinced that women must be controlled by men, so thought Richardson. K. Rogers is quite wrong when she claims that Richardson recognised 'that women have the same potential as men, the same autonomy, the same needs and legitimate claims to self-realisation and self-determination'.[53] He recognised nothing of the sort, and it is wishful thinking to imagine that he did. Whatever a casual reading of Richardson's novels may seem to imply it is likely that he promoted his particular view of women as 'angels' as a means of flattering and educating his audience into 'proper' conduct, according to the ideal which he had painstakingly constructed to illustrate women's moral potential.[54] In one of his private letters Richardson actually used the biblical account of the Fall to justify the subordination of women and made explicit his belief in Eve's culpability: 'It is certain that the Woman's Subordination was laid upon her as a Punishment. And why? — Because *Adam was not deceived* says the Apostle: *but the Woman* being deceived was in the Transgression'. Furthering his case for subordination, Richardson argued that it 'is not a Punishment but to perverse or arrogant Spirits'. Should one reject the above propositions that female subordination was (a) deserved and (b) not really a punishment for good women, then the author would doubtless have employed his trump card: 'Women are safest when dependent'. Safe, because they lacked autonomy. It is no wonder then that Richardson – defender of the ladies – decreed that, for the dear sex 'content is heroism'.[55]

Just as there is 'more than one way to skin a cat' so there is more than one way to subjugate women. Bourgeois moralists such as Richardson – ever ready to formulate principles for others to uphold – sought to control women covertly, by seeking to inculcate norms and values commensurate with the emerging paradigm of woman-hood beloved of the bourgeois male. When commentators such as Kinkead-Weekes refer to Richardson as 'The greatest feminist of the eighteenth century' they fall into the trap of taking Richardson at face value and incidentally betray their ignorance of what consti-tutes feminism.[56] For, having some sympathy with women, enjoying their company and correspondence, and arguing that they should be treated with courtesy and consideration does not make a man a feminist. Richardson did not champion the interests of women as against those of men and did not even think that there was any case for equality between spouses.[57] What Richardson sought was the control of women by men; and for the men themselves to treat women in a more respectful and refined way: men should be well-mannered in their dealings with *ladies*. Perhaps the most liberal attitude that Richardson held regarding women was that they should – given the desire and the talent – be encouraged to greater learning. However he qualified this view by maintaining that 'the great and indispensable duties of women are of the domestic kind', and went on to add that any woman who put learning before these sacred tasks was 'good for nothing'.[58]

Pamela's understanding of the value of chastity has no doubt been influenced by the attitude of her father, whose overwhelming anxiety when he arrives at B— Hall in search of his daughter centres on this very issue: 'Is she honest? Is she virtuous?'. Had she not been, the loving parent would most certainly have disowned her.[59] But Pamela is a determined adherent to the code of feminine virtue, being fully aware of the niceties involved, and needing no cue to make the appropriate judgement against any woman who has trans-gressed. She knows that there *are* women who fail to conform to her standards and asks her parents, 'what sort of creatures must the women-kind be, do you think, to give way to such wickedness?'[60] Pamela defines herself in stark contrast to such women and scorns Mrs Jewkes, who laughs when the heroine solemnly states, 'to rob a

person of her virtue is worse than cutting her throat'.[61] Mrs Jewkes –
who mockingly dubs Pamela 'Purity' – is for Pamela 'a disgrace to
her sex', one who is 'vile and unwomanly', the 'disgrace of woman
kind'.[62] In fact Pamela thinks so ill of her gaoler that she concludes,
'To be sure she must be an atheist'.[63] Nevertheless, although Pamela
remains convinced of Mrs Jewkes's inability to fully reform, she
does eventually forgive her – and even feels some sympathy for that
other erring female, Sally Godfrey, in the light of Sally's suffering
and repentance. Significantly this forgiveness is based upon the
connection that the two women have had with B. rather than anything else.[64]

At various points in the story B. expresses the sort of views which
had been associated with belief in the 'concupiscence' of women; he
implies that Pamela is herself responsible for his own bad conduct
towards her and states, 'she has all the arts of her sex; they were born
with her'. She is, he continues, a 'little witch' and a 'saucy slut', who
is 'perverse' and 'ungrateful'.[65] The image of witchcraft suggests
itself to B. as he endeavours to make sense of Pamela's atypical
attitude; he concludes that she has practised 'insinuating arts' and
has even 'bewitched' Mr Williams: in short, she is a 'sorceress'.[66]

Having found Pamela a match for his scheming and his repartee,
B. bemoans the plight of his own sex, supposing that women have an
unfair natural advantage: 'If our wits were equal to womens' we
might spare much time and pains in our education, for nature teaches
your sex what, in a long course of nature and study, ours can hardly
attain to'.[67] Yet B.'s view of women – in spite of his supposed reformation – does not alter greatly once he has decided to marry Pamela;
he continues to attribute some sort of near-magical power to them:
'The man who thinks a thousand dragons sufficient to watch a
woman, when her inclinations take a contrary bent, will find all too
little: she will engage the stones in the street, or the grass in the field,
to act for her, and help on her correspondence'. B. later tells Pamela,
'Your mind is as pure as that of an angel, and as much transcends
mine', but he continues to be suspicious of women and – after an
altercation with his sister – exclaims, 'Your sex is the d—l; how
strangely can you discompose, and turn, as you please, us poor
weathercocks of men!'[68] For B. whose faults allegedly arise from his
late mother's over-indulgence, even the affair with Sally Godfrey
can be blamed on someone else – namely her mother.'[69] No wonder
then that B. must have complete obedience from his wife; in the first
place he sees such obedience as a right derived from his sex and

status, and in the second, as essential if he is to protect himself and his interests from the ever-present danger represented by women.

However, B. is assured of Pamela's loyalty and obedience. Her fulsome gratitude reaches something of a climax at that point in the marriage service where she is asked if she knows of any impediment which she should reveal; her slavish reply is, 'None, Sir, but my great unworthiness'.[70] After the marriage, when B. gives an impromptu lecture on his likes, dislikes and opinions (with particular reference to married life, child rearing and personal conduct), Pamela responds ecstatically, whimpering, 'pray give me more of your sweet injunctions'.[71] As noted above, the content of this turgid speech is later transformed – by Pamela – into a set of forty-eight rules and propositions which clearly indicate that Pamela is to be the junior partner in the marriage, and that B. will suffer little in the way of contradiction. Yet Pamela is exceedingly happy; her heroic action in the cause of (her) virtue has brought her socio-economic rewards and public recognition of her moral status by her social superiors. She now stands as an example to all women and – in keeping with Richardson's view of what constituted a truly 'feminine' character – would hardly resent being dominated by a man who, she informs us, 'pities my weakness of mind, allows for all my little foibles, and endeavours to dissipate my fears'.[72]

4
Sarah Fielding:
David Simple (1744)

Sarah Fielding's *David Simple* is the story of a young man's quest for a 'real friend' in a society characterised by avarice and injustice. Fielding nowhere suggests that such evils arise from anything other than individual sources, however, and the wrongs which her hero suffers, witnesses or hears of are shown as the consequences of vanity, greed or maliciousness on the part of specific individuals. The question of why so many wicked or morally-lax people exist in the society is not addressed – it is simply implied that they do constitute the majority. Beyond illustrating instances of selfishness, pride and so on, Fielding can only bemoan the world, in which Christian values count for little and almost everyone acts according to their own interests or passions. Given this gloomy picture of society one might wonder why David and his companions do not conform to the pattern of individual wickedness, but no answer is offered other than the notion of individuals having different 'natures'. For Sarah Fielding, some people are good-natured whilst most are not.

Although the author obviously wished to condemn selfish individualism and its consequences, the piece does not constitute an integrated Christian critique of society. So, David's attitudes and actions are not underpinned by a clearly-outlined viewpoint from which he assesses the people and situations he encounters during his search. Rather he somehow conjures up what the author takes to be appropriate feelings 'from the heart', that is, from his innate goodness. This contrasts to some extent with Henry Fielding's *Amelia* wherein, as Alter notes, the problem of adhering to Christian values in a corrupt society is seen as a dilemma not *solely* caused by individual wickedness.[1] In *David Simple* the issue is not so much one of pursuing or maintaining goodness in the face of evil, but more the business of just *surviving* the onslaught of other people's wickedness. As Mullan has pointed out, 'the novel of sentiment in the eighteenth century, committed as it might be to the celebration of fellow-feeling, elaborates pathos from exactly the disconnection of special experiences of sympathy from dominant patterns of social relationship'.[2]

Sarah Fielding offers little in the way of direct comment on religion in her novel; whilst Christianity is held to be desirable and true, specific beliefs are not considered in any detail. This general support for Christianity displays no particular preference for one interpretation over another and shows no prejudice against Catholicism. Two minor characters even find Catholic solutions to their problems, with the approval of David and his friends.[3] David is himself a Christian and is considered by his companions to be an instrument of Providence, yet there is little reference to his imputed beliefs.[4] Camilla's father is also mentioned as a Christian (in spite of the way in which he treats his daughter), the main tenet of his belief apparently being that children should not be subjected to corporal punishment. This supposedly induces servility, something inappropriate in a 'Christian' country where there is no danger of them becoming slaves. However, 'he often added that we did not scruple buying and selling *Slaves* in our Colonies; but then we took care not to convert them to our Faith, for it was not lawful to make *Slaves* of Christians'.[5] This is a good example of formal morality in a character whom Fielding deems generally good – she does not criticise his view on this issue. Yet she has earlier written disdainfully of one aspect of purely formal adherence to religion when commenting upon David's prospective sister-in-law, whose Christianity amounts to weekly church attendance, and who subsequently changes her allegiance in order to marry a wealthy Jew.[6]

At one point in the story we are shown the contrasting character and appearance of a clergyman and an atheist; this allows Fielding to make a crude case against atheism by attributing good qualities to the former and wholly bad ones to the latter. The clergyman is neat, cheerful and plainly dressed whilst the atheist is dirty and unkempt: 'In short, everything without was an Indication of the Confusion within, and he was a perfect Object of Horror'.[7] In the conversation which takes place between these two the atheist speaks out against the vested interests of the clergy and, in the novels of this period, such criticism invariably indicates a bad character: true to form the atheist goes on to proposition Cynthia.[8] In the author's opinion such conduct stems 'from a natural Propensity to Vice': a propensity which we are implicitly invited to attribute to anyone not holding religious beliefs.[9] The discussion between the two revolves around the existence of a deity and the points made by the atheist are quite ineffectual; we do not learn what the minister's allegedly superior rejoinders are. Of course the clergyman only desires 'to do good', and gets the opportunity when the atheist – whilst drunk – breaks a leg.[10] We later learn that this atheist is David's brother, Daniel, and that he has subsequently died as a result of his vices – but not before retracting his disbelief. During his life he had used religion to financially exploit elderly women, his own lack of faith supposedly resulting from his fear of the idea of a deity.[11] Needless to say his life was never happy.

Like Goldsmith, Sarah Fielding appears to have viewed religion as important for its consolatory function; writing against suicide, she illustrates the point with Stainville's recovery, which is dependent upon the fear and consolation provided by religion: it does that 'which no Human help could have done' [12] David sees religion in terms of its soothing powers and, on hearing of the atheist's attempt to refute the proposition that there is a deity, exclaims: 'Good God! is it possible there can be a Creature in the World so much an Enemy to himself, and to all Mankind, as to endeavour to take from Men's Minds the greatest Comfort they can possibly enjoy!'[13] Although there is no adequate apology for religion in *David Simple* it is apparent that Sarah Fielding held conventional and largely uninteresting opinions on the subject.

The author's references to women are in the form of more or less undeveloped observations. That women suffered considerable injustice in the eighteenth century is undisputed, and Fielding lists some examples by presenting a man prepared to sell his daughter, a good wife who is treated abysmally, and an illustration of the lack of compassion (particularly on the part of other women) available for anyone unlucky enough to be 'ruined'.[14] The issue of women's status and lack of power is a recurring theme particularly in relation to marriage and dependency.

On one occasion, when David mixes with the quality, we are shown a young woman who remains silent in company; this incites his curiosity, but Spatter explains, 'it is reckon'd a very ill-bred thing for Women to say any more than just to answer the Questions ask'd them, while they are *single*'.[15] The fact that marriage was a primary aim for virtually all women, with educated women frequently arousing suspicion and disdain, ensures that Cynthia is discouraged from reading anything other than vacuous romances. Her parents tell her:

'Miss must not enquire too far into things, it would turn her Brain; she had better mind her Needle-work, and such Things as were useful for Women; reading and poring on Books, would never get me a Husband'.[16] Given the economic position of most women, few things could be more important than a husband for, as Camilla states, 'good or bad usage was to be had, just according to the situation any person appeared in, and . . . most people weighed the respect they paid others very exactly in a Scale against the Money they thought them worth'.[17]

As Sarah Fielding reiterates, the position of female dependants – of whom there were many in the period – was often unenviable, for a typical 'benefactor','only desired the Wench to *keep her House*, to *take care of her Children*, to *overlook all her Servants*, to be *ready to sit with her when she call'd her*, — with *many more trifling things*'.[18] Cynthia has suffered at the hands of such a patron and tells David, 'People who are so unhappy as to be in a State of Dependance, are forced to do the most nauseous things that can be thought on, to please and humour their Patrons'.[19] Hence the common term for such dependants – 'toad-eaters'. Sarah Fielding was herself dependent upon her brother but there is no evidence that she was ill-used.

Camilla, whose status has declined due to her estrangement from her father, sees her own position as the worst into which anyone could possibly fall: 'Alas, Sir . . . there is no Situation so deplorable, no Condition so much to be pitied, as that of a Gentlewoman in real Poverty. I mean by real Poverty, not having sufficient to procure us Necessaries'.[20] What concerns Camilla here is not that which one might truly consider 'necessary' however – that is, food, shelter, clothing and the like; she is concerned with what is necessary to maintain her *status*. For downward mobility results in a woman being ignored by her friends, propositioned by men, and morally condemned and blamed for her own misfortune. It is this which hurts Camilla. Yet bad as the lot of women such as Cynthia and Camilla may have been, their lives were surely easier than those of the majority of women in Britain at this time – neither of these fictitious women have to resort to whoring, industrial or agricultural labour, or security-oriented marriages.[21]

Sarah Fielding disapproved of such marriages and the general practice of viewing single women as commodities for the marriage market. Cynthia, whose father has tried to force her into an unwelcome alliance, makes it clear that she is opposed to expedient or economically-oriented marriages and goes on to reject the opinion that a wife should be content in the position of an 'upper-a servant', functioning mainly to display her husband's wealth. In her view any woman prepared to marry a fool for financial reasons is in effect prostituting herself. Fielding likewise wants to discredit fortune-hunters of either sex, such as Livia and the atheist (whose exploitation of women is both financial and sexual). In contrast she asserts the importance of mutual love between spouses – something not always considered in a society wherein marriage was often seen as a contract or financial transaction – and the possibility of women being constant in their affections.[22] However, whilst the author argues against wife-beating and other forms of oppression employed by husbands, she also cautions men against indulging their wives to the point of 'spoiling' them. She apparently believed that women, like children, were in need of some external control.[23]

Fielding has something to say about the negative qualities associated with women, but here she simply notes the supposedly feminine vices attributed to women by many other eighteenth-century writers: vanity, envy, inconstancy of affection, encouragement of rakes, coquetry, extravagance and so on.[24] The author's own individualising view of the world ensures that she does not perceive the injustice suffered by women as resulting from structured economic, political or social inequality – once again it is the stupidity and vice of individuals which is to blame. Not surprisingly then, her conception of a good woman is basically the same as that of her male counterparts: someone who conforms to the prototypical feminine virtues of gentleness, obedience, premarital virginity and so on, which – as Needham and Utter have shown – constitute the important characteristics of heroines throughout the English novel from its origins through to the late nineteenth century.[25] In this form the didactic novel constitutes an entertainment in which normative prescriptions and proscriptions are expressed and vicarious emotional gratification is offered to the reader. As Mullan has noted, such novels may portray a harsh and intractable world but the author is 'able to position each private reader as the exceptional connoisseur of commendable sympathies, and to imply such a reader's understanding of the communication of sentiments and the special capacities of sensibility'.[26]

Insofar as Fielding reflects upon rank in *David Simple* she generally adopts the standard poses of the period. David does not believe rank to be the most important factor determining moral worth, but the only character whom he meets who argues against the importance of social position (Orgueil) turns out to be lacking in the most elementary compassion. In practice Orgueil mixes almost exclusively with his own (middle) class and thus the only 'egalitarian' in the story is shown as heartless and, by implication, hypocritical. Unlike Camilla, David is interested in people of lower rank when searching for a real friend – largely because their 'want of Education shewed more openly, and with less disguise, what their Natures were'. However, he finds little to gratify him amongst his social inferiors: 'indeed hitherto his observations of that kind had given him but a melancholy Prospect'.[27]

The stock notions concerning class and status which appear throughout include the conviction that servants are easily corrupted and employers should therefore set them a good example. Nevertheless people at the lower end of the socio-economic scale may be generous in their dealings with others, particularly if those others are destitute; they are also, according to the atheist, more gullible.[28] At the other end of the social continuum we find the upper class whose major vice is –in Fielding's view – their selfishness and superficiality; this is the status-conscious world of fashion and gambling in which the poor, if considered at all, are regarded with the utmost contempt. The men of this class deem their sexually-exploitative attentions towards 'lesser' women a great favour, and to illustrate the point Fielding introduces the archetypal lecherous peer (who in this case partly redeems himself by an altruistic act).[29] Yet in Cynthia's opinion, which I take to be that of the author, the rich and fashionable – with their endless desire for unnecessary and ultimately worthless products – play an important role in the economy. She argues that, given the inequitable distribution of property, (a fact not considered susceptible to change), the lower class – in this instance merchants – can only make a living by catering for the passions of the wealthy.[30] This view amounts to an apology for the vanity and selfishness of the rich and passes without further comment from any of the other characters.

Whilst the aforementioned Orgueil is not presented as a good character, he is not without insight, and is well aware of the favourable way in which money and manners are assessed in comparison to other qualities. However we are later told that the ambitious and the avaricious are not, regardless of what they think, actually happy. They do not have peace of mind – the prerogative of the poor.[31] In spite of some negative comments about the wealthy, Fielding also invites us to disapprove of the allegedly typical attitudes and actions of the poor (she includes an attack on beggars); significantly, the only class who are not in some way badly discredited are the middle class – from which David and his friends are drawn.[32]

Sarah Fielding's contention is that 'human Miseries', 'arise from the Envy and Malignity of Mankind'.[33] The 'solution' which she presents is both conservative and functionalist, a justification for the power of the rich and an admonition to the poor to be content and passive in the face of exploitation and oppression: 'Were all Mankind contented to exert theirs own Faculties for the common Good, neither envying those who in any respect have a Superiority over them, nor despising such as they think their Inferiors; real Happiness would be attainable'. According to Fielding we must simply accept that some are possessed of 'Advantages of Nature, or Station'; this is not to be questioned or challenged (any attempt to do so would be to act from 'envy').[34] The underprivileged are thus instructed to deny their own material interests in the pursuit of altruism whilst the mercenary and self-interested rich are vindicated in their inequitable possession of power and property; it is piously hoped that they might refrain from openly despising those whom they oppress. In her conclusion Fielding writes of the happiness of David and his friends – a state achieved by their having withdrawn from life in the city – and claims that 'it is in the power of every Community to attain it, if every member of it would perform the part allotted him by *Nature*, or his *Station in Life*, with a sincere regard to the Interest of the whole'.[35] In other words, if everyone was 'good' and fulfilled his or her function regardless of what it might be, then everything would be fine. A more direct statement of conservative ideology can hardly be imagined; the author does try to sugar the pill with the notion that all stations are equal and that this should make one satisfied and determined to work 'for the common Good', but the phrase here means little other than the interests of those whose social, political and economic advantages are already well established.[36]

A work such as *David Simple* can only serve to indirectly strengthen the evils which Sarah Fielding felt uneasy about. For the individualist ideology which lay behind the avaricious and self-seeking attitudes which she condemned actually informs her own atomistic view of society. Her conclusion rather glibly implies the comparatively easy achievement of harmony within a communally-oriented society totally unlike the one she has sought to illustrate. Throughout the novel Fielding directs all her efforts towards stressing the

individual sources of good and evil and completely ignores or over-
looks the societal aspect of her subject-matter. Given her account of
human nature, the prescription which she puts forward is quite
invalid; if people can be classified as good or bad 'by nature' – and
nature is itself determined outside of human control – then the
problem is not susceptible to any humanly-constructed remedy. It
could only be resolved by a transformation of human nature by,
presumably, God. Perhaps, as Mullan suggests, such sentimental
novels do not – and indeed do not attempt to – offer a 'practicable
model' of virtue, or really address actual social conditions.[37]

When Sarah Fielding wrote her continuation, *Volume the Last*, the
pessimism which she had displayed in the original work was, if
anything, more deeply held. She confesses her belief 'That solid and
lasting Happiness is not to be attained in this World'.[38] David and his
companions have retreated into the country and enjoyed happiness
for eleven years, but eventually, due to the maliciousness of their old
'friend' Orgueil and some new villains such as Ratcliff, their circumstances go from bad to worse. By the end of this volume only
Cynthia and David's daughter survive and thus Fielding points up
the hopelessness which pervades *David Simple*: the only escape from
a wicked society is the truly individual and transcendent one afforded by death. Given this desperate and mournful account of
social relations it is perhaps not surprising that she produced what
must be one of the most melancholy of all sentimental prose-fictions.

5

Henry Fielding:
Amelia (1751)

One of Henry Fielding's contemporaries, John Cleland, wrote of *Amelia*: 'The chief and capital purpose of this work is to inculcate the superiority of virtuous conjugal love to all other joys'.[1] Conjugal love is certainly an important theme throughout the novel, as Fielding in turn considers feminine virtue, adultery and social corruption. Yet at its simplest *Amelia* is, as Steeves suggests, 'the story of a weak man and a strong woman'.[2]

If Amelia represents the Christian woman of good sense and virtue there are a number of other female characters in the work who are located elsewhere along Fielding's continuum of feminine goodness. And these other women, whom we are tacitly invited to compare to the heroine, all display considerable faults. This may just be a device with which Fielding sought to underline Amelia's exemplary nature, but perhaps it also indicates the somewhat superior attitude which Fielding and most of his contemporaries often displayed towards women. However, given Fielding's didactic purpose in this novel I think that he focuses upon the various failings of his female (and male) characters primarily to criticise particular faults such as selfishness, pride, lechery and so on and I do not agree with K. Rogers that he merely 'accepted the male chauvinism of his culture'.[3]

Nevertheless, we are frequently reminded that Amelia does differ from her fellow women and is a paradigm; in her husband's words, 'the deity I adore'.[4] Predictably her virtues include immense love for her husband and children, chastity, obedience, compassion and the like; this does rather lead Fielding to portray her, as Alter suggests, 'frozen in the conventional poises of virtuous womanhood, a sort of modern version of the Worthy Wife of Proverbs xxxi'.[5]

The most striking contrast to Amelia appears in the character of Miss Matthews; her stance towards the world consists of a mixture of cynicism and overpowering passion – regarding the latter she is both more romantic and egocentric than any of the other females in the work. Her inability or unwillingness to restrain herself, particularly sexually, leads to her seduction, to concubinage, and to attempted murder and adultery; it also causes her to try to wreck Booth and Amelia's marriage. Symptomatically she cares little for 'virtue and religion', which she deems the tools of hypocrisy; in the discussion with Booth wherein this is made clear, it becomes obvious that her notion of love is both selfish and carnal. Thus Miss Matthews represents something of an archetypal wicked woman, being cunning, sensual and completely uninterested in the family unit – a polar opposite to Fielding's heroine, whose very innocence leads her close to snares which the worldly would immediately recognise. Unlike Richardson's Pamela, Amelia is so innocent that it does not occur to her that anyone might attempt her virtue.[6] Miss Matthews considers anyone as ingenuous as Amelia to be a fool, for her own view is that relations between human beings are based upon appearance and mutual deceit whether they occur between members of the same sex or between men and women. In her conversation with Booth she locates the faults of both sexes – but especially those of women – as arising from men: 'I believe that from the damned inconstancy of your sex to ours proceeds half the miseries of mankind', and, 'Oh! Mr. Booth, our sex is d—ned by the want of tenderness in yours'.[7] Nevertheless we never doubt Miss Matthews's ability to look after herself (her very robustness being alien to the model heroine), and *if* she eventually suffers through becoming 'disagreeable in her person and immensely fat', she yet retains power over James, as his mistress.[8] Given Fielding's didactic purpose she escapes rather lightly; as the most reprehensible woman in the piece she has an easier time than, for example, Mrs Bennet (later Atkinson) to whom we now turn.

Mrs Bennet is initially presented to us as a sombre and modest sort of woman, but we soon learn that she is susceptible to vanity. It is this weakness which encourages her to take chances which result in her seduction by the peer who pursues Amelia; the consequences of her earlier misdoings have caused her former husband to commit suicide. However, Mrs Bennet is by no means a wicked woman – in fact it is she who warns Amelia against the lecherous peer and his procuress. But Fielding makes sure that the reader remains aware of her continuing vanity (mainly with respect to her learning) and contrives conversations between her and Dr Harrison to this end. Perhaps Anna Laetitia Barbauld was right when, in considering

Fielding's treatment of Mrs Bennet, she commented, 'Any portion of learning in women is constantly united in this author with something disagreeable',[9] and, 'Mrs. Bennet . . . seems introduced purely to show the author's dislike to learned women'.[10] Quite apart from her vanity, it also transpires that Mrs Bennet is something of a hypocrite; having spoken out strongly against second marriages she herself remarries. And, notwithstanding the high premium which she places upon learning, she states: 'Indeed, I believe that the first wish of our sex is to be handsome'.[11] As the story progresses she puts Amelia's reputation at risk in order to promote her own husband's interests, but it is in her dialogues with Harrison that Fielding presents what he takes to be Mrs Bennet's worst trait.

Dr Harrison, the moral spokesman of the novel, does not – as many commentators have noted – come across as the good-humoured man Fielding leads us to expect, and his sole purpose in speaking with Mrs Bennet appears to be to exercise his contempt for her education. As well as discrediting her via his superior knowledge, Harrison likewise lists some undesirable consequences of female learning which Mrs Bennet's behaviour later confirms. For example, Harrison asks her: 'if a learned lady should meet with an unlearned husband, might she not be apt to despise him?'. Mrs Bennet disagrees yet, in a subsequent and similarly antagonistic encounter with Harrison, her (unlearned) husband ventures an opinion to which she retorts: 'I am sure *you* can be no judge in these matters'.[12] As Battestin notes in his consideration of Fielding's 'good women', 'A true wife, he feels, must attend to the useful domestic duties and must be a good-natured, sensible, and loving companion, yet willing to submit to the superior judgement of her husband'.[13] So when Mrs Bennet refers to 'that nonsensical opinion that the difference of sexes causes any difference in the mind', the author has already done his best to convince us that she is a vain and hypocritical person in spite of her apparent learning.[14] Significantly, Amelia has not had the benefits of a classical education but relies solely upon her own good sense and Christian virtue, plus directives from the two men in her life – Booth and Harrison.

All of the other female characters in *Amelia*, with the exception of Amelia's childhood nurse (Atkinson's mother), are guilty of assorted failings. Amelia's mother is both malicious and snobbish; her sister is envious and tries to swindle the heroine out of her rightful inheritance; her onetime friend, Mrs James, becomes conceited and only values the ceremonial aspect of friendship; her landlady, Mrs Ellison, turns out to be a procuress (as does Mrs Trent) and even Amelia's maid finally deserts her, stealing everything of value in the process. The sheer frequency and diversity of female misdoings in the novel certainly set the heroine apart, as Fielding intended, but do not add to the credibility of her fine example.

Whilst Amelia does occasionally display that weak physical constitution which Watt has described as 'sociosomatic snobbery', her general attitude is characterised by forbearance, cheerfulness and devotion to her wifely duties.[15] The only instance of Amelia (arguably) being in the wrong occurs when she tells Harrison about the duelling challenge sent to her husband by James. Whilst she obviously does not want Booth to put his life at risk she does appreciate that 'honour' demands that he accept the challenge. To this Harrison vehemently retorts:

Honour! Nonsense! Can honour dictate to him to disobey the express commands of his Maker, in compliance with a custom established by a set of blockheads, founded on false principles of virtue, in direct opposition to the plain and positive precepts of religion and tending manifestly to give a sanction to ruffians, and to protect them in all the ways of impudence and villainy?[16]

When Amelia points out that custom and the 'opinion of the world' are perhaps important in this context Harrison shows his disdain for such a view and goes on to remark upon the practice of duelling:

Chiefly, indeed, it hath been upheld by the nonsense of women who, either from their extreme cowardice and desire of protection, or, as Mr. Bayle thinks, from their excessive vanity, have always been forward to countenance a set of hectors and bravoes, and to despise all men of modesty and sobriety; though these are often, at bottom, not only the better but the braver men.

By this time Harrison is so inflamed that he continues long after Amelia has submitted to his opinion; he proceeds to accuse her of a 'desire of feeding passion female vanity with the heroism of her man', and it becomes clear that whatever Amelia says on the subject will be deemed wrong. Drawing upon the example of Andromache dissuading Hector from danger, Harrison concludes, 'This is indeed a weakness, but it is an amiable one, and becoming the true feminine character'; so both dissuasion and encouragement are wrong, but the former is here considered to be more genuinely feminine.[17]

Seduction plays a central part in *Amelia* whether realised – as in the cases of Miss Matthews, Mrs Bennet, and indeed Booth – or merely attempted. Amelia is herself in danger from two of her husband's acquaintances, Bagillard and James, in addition to the mysterious peer. She never appears to appreciate the danger involved, however, as she assumes that 'a woman's virtue is always her sufficient guard'.[18] In case this is interpreted as stupidity Fielding later makes the point that, 'it is not want of sense, but want of suspicion, by which innocence is often betrayed'.[19]

What Fielding here takes to be characteristic of innocence, namely naivety, contrasts markedly with Richardson's view of female innocence as displayed by Pamela. At the very beginning of that saga the heroine's suspicions are aroused via her parents' fears for her virtue, and this ensures that Pamela (although innocent in the practical/sexual sense of the term) is wary in her dealings with B. and his servants. Amelia's innocence is more general and less formal, and Fielding implies that such innocence is at least partly dependent upon her 'naturally' good disposition – although elsewhere in the novel he stresses the importance of a religious education for children and the social forces which contribute to an individual's character: 'it is not from nature, but from education and habit that our wants are chiefly derived'.[20]

The typical seduction theme in eighteenth-century English novels involves a man from the quality pursuing an innocent, middle-class girl; however the emphasis in *Amelia* is upon the adulterous nature of those involved. And insofar as the work can be taken as a limited critique of Fielding's society it is clear that adultery is held to be peculiarly significant. As Alter maintains in his illuminating analysis, 'adultery itself is a kind of paradigm of all that is wrong in a society where Christian values have been discarded'. Furthermore, it is 'the perfect expression of a ruthlessly egoistic hedonism, a cynically exploitative, utterly disengaged relationship to humanity which makes a man willing to inflict all kinds of suffering on others for the sake of his own momentary gratification'.[21] The serious nature of adultery arises from the fact that it not only undermines the relation of husband to wife, but also threatens what Fielding and other Christian writers of the period took to be the primary foundation of society – the family. The kind of selfish individualism which the peer represents is thus contrasted with a more traditional kind of Christian benevolence which begins in the family but also extends to the outside world in the form of charity and brotherly love. Therefore virtuous characters in *Amelia* are less immediately concerned with their own 'state of grace' than their counterparts in Defoe or Richardson. Fielding was himself a Latitudinarian, more concerned with practical Christianity than solitary soul-searching, and as Work has suggested, 'Accordingly his mature life was one of strenuous activity both in the personal practice of Christianity and in the conversion of others to Christian faith and life'.[22]

The fullest denunciation of adultery in the piece appears in Dr Harrison's letter to James, which is by chance found and publicly mocked at the very masquerade where the peer hopes to seduce Amelia. The place is important, for Fielding suggests – via the characters – the morally dubious nature of such entertainments and the corrupt and lax attitudes of those who delight in them.[23] Harrison begins his condemnation by noting the religious law against adultery, but he goes on to claim that it is likewise unnatural and a violation of the husband's property rights: 'If it had not been so expressly forbidden in Scripture, still the law of nature would have yielded light enough for us to have discovered the great horror and atrociousness of this crime'. He continues, 'there is scarce any guilt which deserves to be more severely punished. It includes in it almost every injury and every mischief which one man can do to, or can bring on, another. It is robbing him of his property'.[24] Harrison goes on to argue that the consequences of adultery are likely to include the breaking-up of families, an end to 'industry', disloyalty to King and friends and, perhaps, murder and suicide (Mrs Bennet's first husband being an example of the latter).

Almost all of the action in *Amelia* takes place in London and most historians agree that this was *the* place for instances of (particularly sexual) 'immorality'. Rudé, writing of Hanoverian London, maintains that,

this was a period when public morality and conjugal fidelity, as displayed by the fashionable classes, were at low ebb. Prostitutes openly advertised their wares; gentlemen kept mistresses as a matter of course, if not as a matter of honour: George II set the example (after having been set it, in turn, by his father) by taking his mistress, the Countess of Yarmouth, with him on State visits to Hanover.[25]

In a similar vein Jarrett contends, 'if married women in the labouring classes were made miserable by violence and poverty, those among the aristocracy were made equally miserable by vice and impropriety. Only in the contented ranks of the "middling sort of people" was the paradise for women to be found'.[26]

Given the prevailing attitudes of the rich and fashionable – the frequenters of Vauxhall and Ranelagh, both of which Fielding saw as places of corruption and immorality – it is not surprising that Booth 'was convinced that every man acted entirely from that passion that was uppermost', even though his own behaviour sometimes contradicts this notion.[27] Yet Booth's opinion often finds confirmation within the novel and Harrison, using his own *bête noire* explains why this is to be expected: 'In the great sin of adultery, for instance; hath the government provided any law to punish it? On the contrary, is the most notorious practice of it any detriment to a man's fortune or to his reputation in the world?'. Harrison concludes that the answer to these questions is, 'no', and continues, 'What wonder then if the community in general treat this monstrous crime as a matter of jest, and that men give way to the temptations of a violent appetite, when the indulgence of it is protected by law and countenanced by custom?'[28] This is a form of social criticism, but in spite of the socially-informed observations which appear in the novel, the idea of human nature/natural dispositions to good or evil occurs throughout the narrative. In this respect Fielding seems unable to relinquish one of the ideas which he wished to attack; as Alter points out, in *Amelia* 'the old dichotomy of good and bad nature is partly replaced by another one of human nature and society', but I think that 'partly' should be underlined here for it seems that human nature does, for Fielding, ultimately form the basis of social ills and thus the corrupt society.[29]

However, Fielding considers societal corruption which, in Harrison's words, is 'clogging up and destroying the very vitals of this country'.[30] The law is one of the author's major targets, as he illustrates that bribery is necessary to ensure reasonable treatment from gaolers and bailiffs, and introduces Justice Thrasher who sentences according to his own whim and the apparent status of the unfortunates who appear before him. In Booth's case, 'The justice, perceiving the criminal to be but shabbily dressed, was going to commit him without asking any further questions'.[31] So, money and status determine the quality of justice received from this judge, and it is only because Miss Matthews can provide money that Booth spends so little time in prison. We later learn of the part played by an attorney (Murphy) in swindling Amelia out of her inheritance, and it seems as if almost everyone involved in the process of legal administration is corrupt. Turning to lesser legal functionaries Fielding states, via Dr Harrison, 'there are none whose conduct should be so strictly watched as that of these necessary evils in the society, as their office concerns poor creatures who cannot do themselves justice, and as they are generally the worst of men who undertake it'.[32]

Nevertheless the criticisms made of the legal system are somewhat blunted by the introduction of an upright and honest JP who proceeds to reward the minor villains with their just deserts at the end of the novel. One wonders whether the 'necessary evils' mentioned above are only necessary in an un-Christian society. Fielding sometimes appears to be making such a claim, as when Harrison says:

> The nature of man is far from being in itself evil; it abounds with benevolence, charity, and pity, coveting praise and honour, and shunning shame and disgrace. Bad education, bad habits, and bad customs debauch our nature, and drive it headlong as it were into vice. *The governors of the world, and I am afraid the priesthood, are answerable for the badness of it.* Instead of discouraging wickedness to the utmost of their power, both are to apt to connive at it.[33]

Yet to make any claims – positive or negative – about the 'nature of man' is to employ a paradigm which tends to contradict the author's own 'sociological' pronouncements. I think that Harrison's later discussions of the problem of corruption and the possibility of the 'good' society throw light upon the sources of Fielding's view – and include the assumption that selfishness and disregard for others, not benevolence, characterize the natural disposition of human beings.

In conversation Dr Harrison provides an insight into the author's organic-functionalist perspective: 'corruption of the body politic as naturally tends to dissolution as in the natural body'.[34] This corruption supposedly arises from an improper distribution of functions which, apart from being impractical and harmful to both public and individual well-being, is also morally wrong, for, 'to deny a man the preferment which he merits, and to give it to another man who doth not merit it, is a manifest act of injustice, and is consequently inconsistent with both honour and honesty'.[35] Public and private good 'can never be completed nor obtained but by employing all persons according to their capacities'; this view however does not anticipate Marx, but looks back to Plato's account of the good society as envisaged in his *Republic*.[36] Clearly if it is the 'governors of the world' and the 'priesthood' who are responsible for the corrupt state of society, then one is invited to suppose that if such rulers were good men then a just society could naturally follow (doubtless encouraged by the use of a little force and ideology), as suggested in Plato's vision of the role of the philosopher-king. And in case one is tempted to imagine that Fielding is simply advocating what might currently be termed a 'meritocracy' when he states, 'Wherever true merit is liable to be superseded by favour and partiality, and men are entrusted with offices without regard to capacity or integrity, the affairs of that state will always be in a deplorable condition', it is worth remembering that the best example of modern social organisation was – in his view – that achieved under Cromwell, who, 'carried the reputation of England higher than it ever was at any other time'.[37]

Whilst it is true that Fielding attacked many of the attitudes surrounding class and status which were current in his time, it would be a gross exaggeration to claim that he was – in any contemporary sense – an egalitarian. He did not object to the existence of social differentiation and the unequal distribution of power and money, but rather to the fact that status claims were upheld over and above moral worth and power was frequently misused. The quality attract Fielding's criticism for their conduct, not because élite groups were distasteful to him *per se*. So, whilst the author's attitude towards class and status was less rigid than that of many of his contemporaries, he was not a radical.

The most important working-class character in *Amelia* is Atkinson, who is devoted to the heroine and to Booth; apart from being remarkably virtuous he is also well aware of his place *vis-á-vis* his social superiors. His deferential stance towards Booth is usually accompanied by statements such as, 'I know the distance which is between us'.[38] Every other character is similarly conscious of Atkinson's humble status, and his exemplary conduct is deemed all the more remarkable given his class position. In the course of Booth's conversations with Miss Matthews, Atkinson's generosity is mentioned, causing her some surprise: 'Good heavens! . . . how astonishing is such behaviour in so low a fellow'. To this Booth replies, 'I thought so myself . . . and yet I know not, on a more strict examination into the matter, why we should be more surprised to see greatness of mind discover itself in one degree or rank of life than in another'.[39] Booth goes on to note the frequency of bad conduct amongst the upper classes and the occasional instances of 'whatever is really great and good' to be found amongst their humble counterparts. Later on in the story he remarks, 'there are few who are generous that are not poor', as by now his experience has indicated to him that fairness and altruism are quite alien to the wealthy and powerful.[40]

Even so, there is never any sign that Booth believes that rank can be either ignored or abolished; the point which Fielding wants to make is simply that rank cannot be used as a reliable indicator of the moral worth of any individual. In all of his dealings with Atkinson, Booth does not once treat the former as an equal, nor does he attempt to modify the extreme deference which Atkinson always displays.

Amelia is obviously fond of Atkinson who, she states, has 'great tenderness of heart and a gentleness of manners *not often to be found in any man, and much seldomer in persons of his rank*'. This reference to rank is not appreciated by Atkinson's wife (formerly Mrs Bennet), who retorts; 'And why not in his rank? . . . Indeed Mrs. Booth, we rob *the lower order of mankind* of their due'; predictably she then goes on to stress the importance of education whilst noting that it does not ensure that those who receive it – namely, the upper classes – become particularly virtuous.[41] But the very terms which Atkinson's wife uses suggest that she has not abandoned her concern for class and status, and one doubts whether she would be such a staunch defender of the 'lower orders' were it not for her recent marriage. If additional evidence of her less-than-egalitarian beliefs were required then we have only to consider the comments she has made twenty-four pages earlier. In describing her background to Amelia she recounts how her aunt (another educated yet flawed woman) turned the neighbours against herself and her first husband, 'which is always easy enough to do amongst the *vulgar* against *persons who are their superiors in rank*, and, at the same time, their inferiors in fortune'.[42] Nevertheless Amelia sympathises with the new Mrs Atkinson and herself says, 'How monstrous then . . . is the opinion of those who consider our matching ourselves the least below us in degree as a kind of contamination!'[43] Curiously, Amelia does not appear to have thought about this issue prior to her talk with Mrs Atkinson, in spite of the fact that she too has married a man who is her social inferior.

With regard to women marrying 'downwards' there is no question of Fielding's liberal view being generally held by his contemporaries – it was not; as Watt notes, 'Dr. Johnson . . . regarded it as a "perversion" for a woman to marry beneath her'. Watt then gives his own explanation for this negative attitude (mentioned earlier) which revolves around the idea that women were supposed to be immune to sexual feelings.[44] However, I suspect that Watt's view of the matter accepts too readily an ideological proposition which few men and women of the period actually believed themselves. The important issue behind the objection to women marrying socio-economic inferiors was as follows: given that the predominant eighteenth-century conception involved women – of whatever rank – being obedient and deferential to their husbands, a genteel woman who married, say, an artisan, would necessarily be (in theory at least) under his power. And the ruling class, though unwilling to disrupt this aspect of male dominance, did not relish the prospect of high-status women (and their property) being controlled by men of humble origin.[45]

Mrs Bennet continues her diatribe by arguing that contemporary notions of rank are 'extremely incongruous with a religion which professes to know no difference of degree, but ranks all mankind on the footing of brethren! Of all kinds of pride there is none so contemptible'.[46] Fielding's interpretation of this religiously-oriented 'egalitarianism' was far more literal than that of many other eighteenth-century English writers. Although one might be sceptical as to how far Mrs Atkinson can be seen as a vehicle for Fielding's beliefs here – as he has elsewhere taken pains to discredit her – I think one must conclude that these are his own opinions. Dr Harrison's speech to Amelia (also concerning Atkinson) tends to confirm this:

> I am pleased with the behaviour of you both to that worthy fellow, in opposition to the custom of the world; which, instead of being formed on the precepts of our religion to consider each other as brethren, teaches us to regard those who are a degree below us, either in rank or fortune, as a species of beings of an inferior order in the creation.[47]

It is Fielding's belief in a common humanity which provides the basis for any 'egalitarianism' displayed in the work and not, of course, a conviction that individuals should be equal in a political context. For, apart from the corruption of the quality, the thing which the author really wishes to attack is not class dominance and privilege but rather snobbery. Fielding's view on this is demonstrated by the example of Mrs James who, having married a wealthy man, forgets the true nature of friendship and acts towards Amelia with decorum but no real feeling. Moreover the benevolence which Fielding believes to be appropriate when dealing with the lower orders, itself tends towards a form of paternalism; equality can only be such in the eyes of God.

Amelia is certainly not proud, or guilty of assessing people on the basis of rank; not only does she suffer from marrying downwards, but when Booth's situation becomes so bad that he decides to follow Harrison's advice and take up farming, 'She was so kind as to say that all stations of life were equal to her, unless one afforded her more of my company than another'. Likewise Amelia maintains that 'none deserve happiness, or indeed, are capable of it, who make any particular station a necessary ingredient'.[48] In spite of this Booth sees the move as one which compromises his status. Amelia later reaffirms her beliefs when she states: 'I would not be ashamed of being the wife of an honest man in any station', and from what we have learnt of her character we are inclined to take this claim at face value.[49] Towards the close of the novel when the couple's fortunes are at their lowest point, Booth asks his wife, 'How shall we live?' And Amelia's immediate reply is, 'By our labour. . . I am able to labour, and I am sure I am not ashamed of it'. She adds, 'why should I complain of my hard fate while so many who are much poorer than I enjoy theirs? Am I of a superior rank of being to the wife of the honest labourer? Am I not a partaker of one common nature with her?'.[50] Noble as this seems it is nonetheless true that Amelia has never experienced any work worth mentioning (even during their hardest times the couple keep a maid); Fielding was not about to let her start at this stage.

Perhaps as Price suggests,

Fielding can reward his heroes because they do not seek a reward. He wishes to free our faith in order, as Pope does, from any simple-minded expectation that goodness will find its reward on earth. The only reward it can find there is that it pays to itself: the pleasure it finds in doing good and in sustaining its integrity.[51]

However if Price is right about the author's intention one might conclude that in this respect Fielding has failed, for the conclusion of *Amelia* – in which villains are punished and the good rewarded – seems to me to reinforce this 'simple-minded expectation'.

6

Oliver Goldsmith:
The Vicar of Wakefield (1766)

Goldsmith's *The Vicar of Wakefield* traces the fortunes of a rural clergyman and his family in a manner which alternates between the comic and the apparently serious. There is some disagreement as to how far Goldsmith intended his main character, Dr Primrose, to be a satirical figure, but, whilst not wishing to enter into that controversy, I am treating the novel as non-satirical insofar as it deals with issues such as politics and religion. Although certain incidents and actions are clearly supposed to be humorous, Goldsmith generally treats political and religious notions as important rather than amusing. The novel was taken at face value by Goldsmith's contemporaries and was frequently praised for the high moral tone which reviewers appear to have discovered in the work. This in itself provides some justification for approaching it as a serious piece; the author's intention (even if one accepts that Goldsmith was as sophisticated as Hopkins suggests) is merely one factor to be considered. In a sociological study of literature intention must always be balanced against the overall social context of the work, including the response of readers and critics, as this remains a more reliable indicator of the work's social relevance.[1]

The basic plot of the novel concerns the vicissitudes faced by the Vicar and his family; these consist of a series of misfortunes, usually arising from the Vicar's naive and over-optimistic stance towards the world, and include a lost fortune, confidence tricks, a broken engagement, a seduced daughter and a domestic fire. Apart from the Vicar himself, characters include good and bad aristocrats, wise and foolish daughters, a status-seeking, money-grabbing wife, a penitent villain and others. Firstly we can examine the author's presentation of female characters; I would suggest that Goldsmith displays a consistent and systematically negative view of them in particular and of women in general.

Family life is an important subject in *The Vicar of Wakefield*, being
one of Primrose's major preoccupations; he is comically dogmatic –
as a strict 'monogamist' – on the issue of marriage, and frequently
speaks at length about his children.[2] However he sees no need to be
involved in the day-to-day running of the household; whilst his wife
and two daughters perform domestic tasks (practical labour) he
concentrates – apart from a little agricultural dabbling – upon spiritual work: 'The temporal concerns of our family were chiefly committed to my wife's management; as to the spiritual, I took them
entirely under my own direction'.[3] In fact he does not fulfil his
responsibilities here, as his lax attitude towards his children – and
the consequences of this – later prove. Although the Vicar's wife,
Deborah, is held responsible for all things pertaining to the household, there is never any doubt (regardless of the Vicar's frequent
stupidity) as to who is the more intellectually able of the two, at least
not in Primrose's mind. And, in spite of the fact that Deborah often
disobeys her husband, the power structure within the family obviously favours the Vicar.

As far as he is able Primrose calls the tune, and even has an
epitaph for his (living) wife which supposedly helps to keep her on
the right track: 'It admonished my wife of her duty to me, and my
fidelity to her; it inspired her with a passion for fame, and constantly
put her in mind of her end'.[4] Even in this short epitaph one can see
that whilst Deborah has a *duty* to her husband (i.e. he has rights), in
return she has nothing more than a promise of his fidelity. Additionally the epitaph employs the notion that her vanity or 'passion for
fame' is a strong incentive to compliant behaviour, as is the re-
minder of her 'end'. Throughout, Deborah is shown to be motivated
by a desire to improve herself and her family via her daughters, a
wise marriage or two being seen as the solution to the problem of
inadequate finances and lowered status. Her status pretensions are
underlined shortly after Burchell saves Sophy's life, for the Vicar
tells us: 'If he had birth and fortune to entitle him to match into such
a family as ours, she knew no man she would sooner fix upon'.[5] As
the reader already knows, and as the Vicar reiterates, the position of
the family is such that any aloofness of this kind is laughably inappropriate; however Primrose soon adopts a similar attitude.

Primrose's family is, in his words, 'The little republic to which I
gave laws'; this does not point – as the term 'republic' might imply
– towards the Puritan conception of the family, but rather indicates

the more general patriarchal assumptions behind the Vicar's outlook. It may well be ironic too, for the laws are not always complied
with.[6] In' many respects the Vicar's stance towards his wife and
daughters – which reflects the views of Goldsmith, with his Tory-
Anglican sympathies – is extremely patronising. For example, when
Deborah and the girls spend time on their appearance the Vicar
lectures them on vanity and mocks them in a manner which encourages the reader to adopt his superior pose. It is also worth noting
that – in the exchange which takes place between the couple at this
point – the Vicar refers to Deborah by the term 'child'; women and
children were often seen to occupy roughly the same position in the
social structure as far as status and rights were concerned, and given
the position of eighteenth-century English women this view was not
always far from the truth.

The arrival of Primrose's landlord, Squire Thornhill, allows the
Vicar further scope for his negative observations; whilst he remains
wary of the Squire, at least two of the women are favourably im-
pressed by what he terms 'the power of fortune and fine clothes'.[7]
The situation also provides Primrose with an opportunity to deline-
ate the 'contrariness' of women; having learnt that one daughter,
Sophy, says nothing against Thornhill, whilst the other, Olivia, claims
to dislike him, the Vicar states: 'I found by this, that Sophia inter-
nally despised, as much as Olivia secretly admired him'.[8] Primrose,
ever aware of status differences, had earlier made a half-hearted
attempt to discourage any relationship between the Squire and his
daughters, feeling that 'such disproportionate acquaintances' are
harmful; in this instance he turns out to be right.[9] However the Vicar
makes no serious effort to hinder Thornhill's pursuit of Olivia and it
is likely that Goldsmith wanted the reader to recognise this as a
failing on Primrose's part.

It is obvious that Thornhill is a bad character, for it is signalled by
his comments against the Church; these lead the Vicar to muse, 'I
could have been better pleased with one that was poor and honest,
than this fine gentleman with his fortune and infidelity'.[10] In this the
Vicar is deceiving himself, as when Sophy shows her regard for
Burchell, Primrose remarks, 'nor could I conceive how so sensible a
girl as my youngest could thus prefer a man of broken fortune to one
whose expectations were much greater'. This is followed by the
Vicar's reflection that: 'as men are capable of distinguishing merit in
women, so the ladies often form the truest judgments of us. The two
sexes seem placed as mutual spies upon each other, and are fur-
nished with different abilities, adapted for mutual inspection'.[11]

Notwithstanding the Vicar's own naivety, much of the novel centres around his sceptical observations upon the pretensions and naivety of his wife and daughters; although he has reservations about the exact status of the two 'ladies' introduced to the family by the Squire, 'My daughters seemed to regard their superior accomplishments with envy; and what appeared amiss, was ascribed to tip-top quality breeding'.[12]

The whole issue of his daughters' pretensions and aspirations causes the Vicar some anxiety, for 'their breeding was already superior to their fortune; and . . . greater refinement would only serve to make their poverty ridiculous, and give them a taste for pleasures they had no right to possess'.[13] This last statement is made to Thornhill when the issue of how London would 'improve' the girls is raised by the Squire's whores; Thornhill goes on to make his 'basest proposal' to Primrose (who is already unhappy at the idea of the girls going to London), and when the Vicar shows his indignation, the Squire simply denies the implication of his own words. This denial is readily accepted by the Vicar and shortly afterwards he endorses the idea of his daughters going to the city for two (fictitious) jobs spoken of by the Squire's accomplices. The motive behind his compliance is that the family could use the money and, moreover, 'if the Squire had any real affection for my eldest daughter, this would be the way to make her every way qualified for her fortune'.[14] So, the unworldly Dr Primrose is aware of the benefits of his daughter making a good match and – in the light of the possible financial advantage to be gained – forgets his former caution and concern for his daughters' safety and virtue. Nevertheless the Vicar's hope that his daughter(s) might be a solution to pecuniary problems does not prevent him from continuing to lecture on the folly of cross-class relationships: 'Unequal combinations are always disadvantageous to the weaker side, the rich having the pleasure, and the poor the inconvenience that result from them'.[15] But the Vicar does not appear to believe his own rhetoric, for he completely ignores Burchell's warnings against the girls going to London and, referring to Burchell, states to Sophia: 'It would be even madness to expect happiness from one who has been so very bad an economist of his own'.[16] In other words the Vicar is not prepared to consider Burchell (whom he knows to be a good man) as a potential suitor for his youngest daughter. His reasons are solely financial.

Apart from the ever-present 'vanity' ascribed to the women in the novel, the central theme relating to women is that of feminine virtue – which is little more, as far as Goldsmith's view of unmarried women is concerned, than the equation of virginity with virtue. When Olivia disappears the Vicar says to his children, 'all our earthly happiness is now over! Go, my children, go and be miserable and infamous; for my heart is broken within me!'[17] Olivia's virginity (which Primrose immediately assumes to be lost) is taken to be of such importance that he can go on to moan, '*Had she but died!* But she is gone, the honour of our family is *contaminated*, and I must look for happiness in other worlds than here'.[18] So here we have a view of unmarried women which deems their sole worth to be dependent upon one thing – is she a virgin? When the 'wretched delinquent' is found by her father and they return home, Deborah takes it upon herself to give Olivia a hard time. By now the Vicar's horror has been assuaged, but he is not surprised by the difficulty of a reconciliation between the girl and her mother, for 'women have a much stronger sense of female error than men'.[19] All that this signifies is that Deborah has accepted the dominant view of the nature of sexuality and its place in estimating the moral qualities of any particular woman. If women are taught to see physical chastity as the main indicator of their worth (and likewise of their life-chances) then it is hardly surprising that many of them may come to place as much – or more – emphasis upon the issue of female sexual purity than men. In eighteenth-century England such 'purity' had considerable economic, religious, and social implications. And, if one uncritically embraces dominant ideas such as those surrounding sexual purity, one will be severely restricted when trying to understand the true nature of phenomena deemed morally wrong within such a framework. The fact that the notions employed by Deborah can act as oppression against her does not modify her endorsement of them; this is not unusual, whether in the context of female oppression or in wider areas. The phenomenon of the oppressed wholeheartedly legitimating a system of exploitation and oppression can be located throughout history. Often such accommodation evolves out of the strategies which the oppressed employ as a means of self-protection, but this conscious or expedient mode of responding to particular contexts and situations may become replaced (if only gradually) by a more fundamental incorporation of the *Weltanschauung* held by the oppressors.

Of course Olivia suffers for her violation of normative sexual rules, even to the point of physical decline, and, having lost her 'unblushing innocence', 'Anxiety now had taken strong possession of her mind; beauty began to be impaired with her constitution, and neglect still more contributed to diminish it'.[20] This is no doubt exacerbated by her mother's tactless request for her to recite the following classic piece of misogynistic verse:

> When lovely woman stoops to folly,
> And finds too late that men betray,
> What charm can sooth her melancholy?
> What art can wash her guilt away?
>
> The only art her guilt to cover,
> To hide her shame from every eye,
> To give repentance to her lover,
> And wring his bosom, is — to die.[21]

This is a reiteration of the 'had she but died!' sentiment expressed by the Vicar. The idea that a woman's loss of virginity prior to marriage requires atonement may seem absurd to the modern reader, but the view that it requires her death was extreme even by eighteenth-century standards (although Richardson employed death to cure dishonour for the eponymous heroine of *Clarissa*). I have yet to find an example of such a drastic punishment/cure befalling a hero who loses his (hetero)sexual innocence. Whilst any woman who lost her virginity before marriage had to deal with guilt and shame, according to Goldsmith, he apparently thought that it was enough – perhaps more than enough – for her male counterpart or seducer simply to repent. This sort of view is not even in keeping with Christianity as I understand it; no matter, neither secular nor religious sophistry can disguise the callousness or vindicate the misogyny of Goldsmith's trite little poem.

When Thornhill offers to have Olivia married-off to someone else it is the Vicar's wife and daughters who argue that this solution should be accepted: they crumble under the threat of economic pressure which the Squire outlines, whilst Primrose remains firm against condoning 'adultery'. This is just one more example of the way in which the women of the novel are portrayed as being morally inferior to the central character; at one point Primrose even refers to Olivia as 'the cause of all our calamities' and this, as he later admits, is really not true.[22] Indeed many of the problems which beset the family are a direct result of the Vicar's own folly. Having said this it must be remembered that the Vicar – for all his faults – is consistently presented to the reader as a good man. And his stupidity is invariably surpassed by that of his wife. During his spell in prison Primrose finds that his wife and daughters believe that prisoners cannot bè reformed, and therefore do not merit the attention of a clergyman. And, if another example of feminine misjudgment were required, we then learn that Deborah has persuaded her eldest son to issue a duelling challenge to the Squire. Later, when Burchell again reprimands the son, George, on the subject of duelling, he is quick to forgive him upon discovering that the blame lies primarily with Deborah; her mistake being just the sort of thing one might 'expect' from a woman. Nevertheless Burchell – who has supposedly been looking for a woman who will want him for himself rather than his money – eventually condescends to marry Sophia. The transaction between the Vicar and the aristocrat occurs after the latter has saved the girl from her abductors; the clergyman states: 'And now, Mr Burchell, as you have delivered *my girl*, if you think her a recompense, *she is yours*'.[23] The fact that Sophia wants Burchell does not alter the nature of the arrangement, nor the underlying assumption that she belongs to the Vicar – that is, she is his property to bestow upon whomsoever he deems appropriate.

It finally transpires that Thornhill has (unwittingly) legally married Olivia, and the Vicar is delighted with this news, for 'she was now made an honest women of'.[24] This is perhaps the clearest example in the work of the formal and vacuous conception of virtue employed throughout; the fact of Olivia having been married prior to her loss of virginity solves the problem, regardless of any other considerations. Fortunately this knowledge effects an immediate improvement in Olivia's health and morale: 'To be thus restored to reputation, to friends, and fortune at once, was a rapture sufficient to stop the progress of decay, and restore former health and vivacity'.[25] But Thornhill suffers the ultimate blow at this point, for Burchell allows him merely a 'bare competence', and charges Olivia with the control of one third of the miscreant's fortune. They do not, however, live happily ever after, but continue to live apart.

Much has been made of the idea that Goldsmith was against the conception of romantic love/marriage held by many of his contemporaries, and it has been suggested that he preferred a more 'realistic' approach to the topic.[26] However it would be absurd to claim that *The Vicar of Wakefield* is a particularly realistic novel – it is, as Allen argues, comparable to a 'fairy-tale'.[27] And, notwithstanding Goldsmith's supposed scepticism about marriage, it is significant that marriage is the climax of the novel: it is used as a logical conclusion to the story. Judging by Goldsmith's comments elsewhere on the subject of marriage it appears that his main purpose was to advocate what he took to be 'rational' love, based upon character before anything else. Unfortunately this 'rational' approach as displayed in the novel seems to involve a good deal of misogyny; as A. Lytton Sells has remarked, 'In few novels are women more cruelly derided'.[28]

Throughout the novel Goldsmith uses Primrose to present the idea that low status (and its corollaries of low income and harsh conditions) is as fortunate as high status. The Vicar makes rather silly comments such as, 'the poor live pleasantly', in his bid to take the sting out of the downward mobility which he and his family have suffered; such misconceptions are frequently found amongst those who prosper.[29] Yet the Vicar's remarks are not solely concerned with morale-boosting, as we shall see below when he attempts to prove the 'equal dealings of Providence'.[30] The family do not have to endure the kind of poverty one might expect from some of Primrose's observations, for they still fare well enough to retain a servant. And even in their comparative poverty, 'we began to find that every situation in life may bring its own peculiar pleasures'.[31] It is in this position that Primrose speaks out against 'disproportionate friendships' and 'fortune hunting', and thus seeks to discourage his family from seeking intimacy with Thornhill. Additionally, when one of Primrose's sons seeks to defend the Squire – suggesting that he cannot be blamed for his mistaken views – the Vicar completely rejects this thesis and issues a brief statement of extreme voluntarism: 'though our erroneous opinions be involuntary when formed, yet, as we have been wilfully corrupt or very negligent in forming them, we deserve punishment for our vice or contempt for our folly'.[32] This sort of view attempts to locate all responsibility and all determinations *within* the individual and demonstrates a total lack of awareness of the role of social structure/process in shaping beliefs and actions. It can be used to provide ready-made explanations for individual character flaws, or to explain away structural problems such as widespread poverty. But this puerile outlook fails on every count; it does not even seem to allow for genuine mistakes (not that this applies in Thornhill's case) or consider factors such as lack of information, inability to discern and so on.

Primrose tries to foster the impression that it is only his wife and daughters who hold status aspirations (although this is clearly not so), and it is significant that Burchell – the 'good' aristocrat – shows his contempt for all such pretensions on a number of occasions, particularly in response to the talk of the 'ladies' who impress Deborah and her daughters. Yet the Vicar is left wondering how to deal with the fact that one of his daughters is sought by one much above her in rank, whilst the other is admired by one who appears to have a lower status than the Primrose family.

The most overt presentation of political ideology in the novel occurs when the Vicar – searching for his daughter, Sophia – is taken to the home of a 'well-dressed gentleman'. This character proves to be an advocate of 'liberty', supporting the power of Parliament rather than that of the king. Goldsmith/Primrose wants to make a case for the king and the middle class, whilst propounding a kinder-garten form of transcendental egalitarianism. Not surprisingly then, he introduces the notion that, although the king is a 'sacred power', 'We have all naturally an equal right to the throne: we are all origi-nally equal'.[33] What 'originally' refers to here is not clear; in discuss-ing the Levellers the Vicar argues that 'it is entailed upon humanity to submit, and some are born to command and others to obey'.[34] This is the old chestnut commonly dragged out to provide an apology for inequality and exploitation, the idea of innate abilities and human nature determining who leads and who is led. According to Prim-rose's tendentious account, the Levellers' project failed because 'there were some among them stronger, and more cunning, than others, and these became masters of the rest'.[35] In fact the Levellers were suppressed by Cromwell. It is worth noting that the form of egali-tarianism attacked here by Goldsmith would not begin to fulfil what one might take as minimal conditions for 'equality' nowadays.

Having argued for the sacred nature of kingship, Primrose goes on to contradict the notion by claiming that the 'generality of man-kind', 'have unanimously created one king, whose election at once diminishes the number of tyrants, and puts tyranny at the greatest distance from the greatest number of people'.[36] This implies – wrongly – that kingly power is based upon consensus, and is the result of (presumably secular) 'election'. Moreover it promotes the sophistic propositions that monarchy erases local tyranny, and that geographi-cal and social distance lessens the possibility of tyranny being char-acteristic of the rule of monarchy. Goldsmith then sets about making his pleas for the middle class, firstly by attacking the 'great' or aristocracy; the assumption here is that the interests of the latter class lie in undermining the power of the monarch, aristocratic am-bition being fuelled by the accumulation of wealth. After some fatuous harping upon this subject, the Vicar bemoans the disappearance of feudalism (a process which was itself a precondition for the emergence of the bourgeoisie), and speaks out against laws which tend to encourage accumulation, and by which, 'the natural ties that bind the rich and poor together are broken'.[37] Just what these 'natural ties' consisted of is left unexplained. However, Primrose goes on to claim that the wealthy invariably gather 'slaves' around themselves and that the only class free from servitude – whilst not possessing great affluence – is the middle class: 'that order of men which subsists between the very rich and the very rabble; those men who are possessed of too large fortunes to submit to the neighbouring man in power, *and yet are too poor to set up for tyrants themselves*'.[38] So here Goldsmith is admitting that the rule of a monarch does *not* prevent localised tyranny; the underlined section is noteworthy for it points up the conservative belief that human beings are naturally selfish and unjust – there is no suggestion that even the admirable middle class would be anything other than tyrants, given the means to be so. Goldsmith maintains that the bourgeoisie are the most important section of society: 'In this middle order of mankind are generally to be found all the arts, wisdom, and virtues of society. This order alone is known to be the true preserver of freedom, and may be called THE PEOPLE'.[39] Goldsmith virtually equates the middle class with 'society' – a comparatively small number of the population are here seen as the creators of all that is decent and worthwhile; they are flanked on one side by a few avaricious aristocrats and on the other by the unruly yet largely inconsequential 'rabble'.

The Vicar opposes any extension of political rights for the above mentioned rabble (that is, the vast majority of the population), as he feels that this would 'drown' the voice of the bourgeoisie; he argues that if the rabble were given any part in political life they would act as they were told to by the wealthy:

> In such a state, therefore, all that the middle order has left, is to preserve the prerogative and privileges of the one principal governor with most sacred circumspection. For he divides the power of the rich, and calls off the great from falling with tenfold weight on the middle order placed beneath them.[40]

This paints a totally false picture of the socio-political reality of Goldsmith's period, assuming as it does that the monarch acted as an impartial arbitrator and in this way 'administered' society. But using this false premise Primrose adds: 'if there be anything sacred amongst men, it must be the annointed SOVEREIGN of his people; and every diminution of his power, in war or peace, is an infringement upon the real liberties of the subject'.[41] Given this rosy view of the king, and the idea that the middle order constitute the people, the Vicar concludes that he has made a case for freedom. But he has simply made a case for the monarch and the bourgeoisie, and a poor one at that. At this point in the story it is revealed that Primrose's listeners are actually servants; one supposes that this device is employed to discredit the anti-monarchist position which they represent.

A remarkable example of the Vicar's own bourgeois moralising and political posturing occurs when he is led to believe that his eldest daughter has been married to Thornhill by a priest who had officiated at the Squire's previous 'marriages'. Olivia tells her father that she has sworn not to reveal the name of this priest – thus protecting him against prosecution – and the Vicar, notwithstanding the way in which his daughter has been used and the danger remaining for others, confirms that she must keep her promise, for, 'Even though it may benefit the public, you must not inform against him. In all human institutions a smaller evil is allowed to procure a greater good; as, in politics, a province may be given away to secure a kingdom; in medicine, a limb may be lopped off to preserve the body; but in religion the law is written, and inflexible, *never* to do evil'.[42] Presumably the Vicar takes his daughter's case to be in the realm of religion because (a) it involves marriage – a 'sacred' institution – and (b) because to break a vow would be a further sin for her. So, even though disclosure may serve to protect others, Primrose urges Olivia to do that which he sees as best for *her* spiritual well-being. Primrose's reasoning on this topic underlines the formal and empty nature of his stance and typifies a type of diminished Christianity which – quite apart from separating religion from every other sphere of life – locates religion *solely* within the individual and thus signifies a retreat from both the Catholic position and its immediate successors in radical Protestantism. It is a peculiarly modern/ bourgeois view of Christianity, ethics and so on, involving the 'privatisation' of issues previously seen as being of social concern and relevance; here the individualism of Protestantism has become inward-looking and passive towards the outside world.[43]

Another example of the Vicar's formal conception of right and wrong occurs when he is arrested and 'the poor' attempt to rescue him. He turns upon them and asks, 'Is this the manner you obey the instructions I have given you from the pulpit?'.[44] Rebuking his parishioners, he goes on to demonstrate that – regardless of the dangerous practical consequences which could rebound upon them – he himself accepts the 'justice' of his arrest, and is horrified that they can even countenance rising up against *legal authority*. Such formalism rules out any action against those in power (whether they are just or otherwise) for the fact of power is taken to be its own vindication.

Once inside the prison, Primrose meets Jenkinson (a con-man who has previously robbed the Vicar and his son), who now bemoans his criminal past: 'Ah, Sir! had I but bestowed half the pains in learning a trade that I have in learning to be a scoundrel, I might have been a rich man at this day'.[45] This is the 'honesty is the best policy' line; it ignores the fact that people do not always have the choice of whether or not to learn a trade, or even to secure the most humble of jobs. The implicit claim behind it is that criminal acts arise from purely individual determinations, and therefore crime cannot usefully be seen as structured (and indeed generated) by particular social formations. One is left with the idea that 'criminals' are simply wicked and anti-social, and never merely struggling to survive within hostile circumstances (in this case the ruthless process of industrialisation). Characteristically, the Vicar has no idea of the availability and rewards of wage-labour; this is made patently obvious when he suggests that his son, George, will be able to support the family (of five adults and two children) with what he can earn as a 'day-labourer'.[46] Nevertheless Jenkinson continues to reflect upon his own criminal activities and argues that to be 'suspicious' of strangers retards one's success in the world; he appears to be advocating some form of romantic naivety as preferable to circumspection: perhaps he supposes the Vicar to be a representative of the former. Jenkinson explains that he became involved in crime because he was considered to be 'cunning' and was therefore 'obliged to turn sharper in my own defence'.[47] This is possibly the least plausible account of criminalisation one is likely to find anywhere in the English novel; in comparison, Defoe's implicit explanation of the phenomenon in *Roxana* and *Moll Flanders* is eminently realistic.

Primrose's decision to try to reform his fellow-prisoners meets with 'universal disapprobation' from his family, who believe that such a project is both impossible and sure to 'disgrace' the Vicar's 'calling'. However, he braves the disapproval of his family and the jests of his audience; consequently, 'My design succeeded, and in less than six days some were penitent, and all attentive'. He even manages to organise some small-scale commodity production and applies/administers a system of social control based upon rewards and punishments: 'Thus in less than a fortnight I had formed them into something *social and humane,* and had the pleasure of regarding myself as a legislator, who had brought men from their *native ferocity* into friendship and obedience'.[48] The ideas behind Primrose's reform include the need for organised work to occupy the physical and mental capacities of men (women are nowhere mentioned in relation to reform), the use of both positive and negative sanctions to ensure that discipline prevails, and the conviction that – in the absence of firm leadership and guidance – men will naturally act like 'animals'. It is their 'native ferocity' which must be transformed into something 'social and humane'. This is just the sort of negative picture of human nature which one would expect from Tory-Anglicans then and now.

Assertions about any fixed characteristics attributable to human nature are beset with problems; such pronouncements are often justified by reference to 'empirical reality', but can typically be countered with alternative examples. The conviction that human nature is essentially good – or that it is basically evil – is nothing more than speculation based upon unproven beliefs. And the supposition that clichés such as 'it's human nature' explain anything is completely misguided; such phrases only mystify and fix dispositions, potential and so on in an invalid manner. Notions of a fixed (good or bad) human nature are frequently employed in ideologies – and in forms of 'common sense' – which represent the interests of those who have something to gain or preserve by arguing for a static human nature. Apologies for existing power relations usually refer implicitly or explicitly to human nature; quite bluntly, there is no such thing as human nature in the usually accepted sense of the term. Human beings have various potentials and limitations, but the extent to which these determine their lives is (with some important exceptions) historically specific; it is only through the course of history that human capabilities are realised, and that which may be impossible in one epoch may be possible – or even commonplace – in another. The way that actual human beings act and reason is the result of a number of factors, but even the most sparse knowledge of history shows the flexible character of human existence. To generalise or universalise examples of human behaviour as somehow epitomising human nature is to run the risk of assuming particular historical phenomena to be omni-historical and omni-cultural. Mészáros sums up what I take to be the most fruitful view of human nature: 'man must be described in terms of his needs and powers. And both are, equally, subject to change and development. Consequently there can be nothing fixed about him, except what necessarily follows from his determination as a natural being, namely that he is a being with *needs* – otherwise he could not be called a natural being – and *powers* for their gratification without which a natural being could not possibly survive'.[49]

Now the Vicar wants to argue that reform – as opposed to severity – is the most useful way of dealing with miscreants, yet whilst he speaks against punishment being made 'familiar' he also states that it should be made more 'formidable'. If this means anything other than making it more severe then the Vicar does not tell us what his alternative to severity is. He goes on to question the use of capital punishment for crimes against property; this is interesting as it reflects Goldsmith's rejection of (or confusion regarding) bourgeois property rights. In a remarkable piece of sophistry Goldsmith argues via Primrose that, for example, a stolen horse is as much the property of the thief as of the previous owner. This and other bizarre propositions are supposedly vindicated by reference to 'natural law', something which Primrose imagines to be demonstrated in the lives of savages: 'Savages, that are directed by natural law alone, are very tender of the lives of one another; they seldom shed blood except to retaliate former cruelty'.[50] Quite apart from the invalidity of the specific pseudo-anthropological claim being made here, it is perhaps worth stating that any notion of natural law remains abstract and open to serious objection. Laws are made by human beings, not given by gods or determined by nature; any laws employed by any people are socially constructed.

Goldsmith was right to attack the fact of property being valued above human life and the ready use of capital punishment available within English law as it then stood, but his argument is so inadequate as to ensure few converts. He fails to locate the real reasons for the fetishism surrounding property and likewise the reasons for its unequal distribution; all he discerns is the way in which the sanctity of property was reinforced by the punishment of anyone who violated it. The Vicar can only conclude that increased wealth leads to a greater fear of loss on the part of the wealthy which in turn encourages them to create more laws (which in their turn produce more 'vices'). It is true that Primrose believes that criminals may be susceptible to reform, but this amounts to little more than a vague hope given that he has no proper account of the causes of crime. The idea of reform here rests upon the pious Christian belief that – in spite of the wicked nature of human beings – 'few minds are so base as that perseverance cannot amend'; there is also a pragmatic design behind the Vicar's apparently humane attitude towards offenders for they 'might, if properly treated, serve to sinew the state in times of danger'.[51] In other words they can risk their lives for the interests of the rich and powerful even though they themselves must not be allowed basic social or political rights. Primrose/Goldsmith has more to say on the issue of politics but as it is so intertwined with religious ideology I will consider it below.

The Vicar's religious opinions are scattered throughout the novel and offer no surprises; in the main these views are presented in a serious manner. Primrose's major exposition is to be found in Chapter XXIX. Here he endeavours to show the 'equal dealings of Providence', starting with the claim that whilst there is much suffering in the world, one can only endure it. There is no suggestion that anything at all can be done to change this sorry state of affairs or even to narrow the gap between the 'fortunate' and the 'wretched'. Moreover we cannot even know why suffering occurs for, 'On this subject, Providence has thought fit to elude our curiosity, satisfied with granting us motives to consolation'.[52] Given the Vicar's beliefs it follows that consolation is the *only* means by which suffering can be modified. Here, according to Primrose, religion is far superior to philosophy (which he considers to be riddled with contradictions) as the former 'comforts in a higher strain. Man is here, it tells us, fitting up his mind, and preparing it for another abode'. Obviously the Vicar is propounding transcendentalism and claiming that human life is essentially unimportant in itself; it is only significant as a stage prior to 'heaven'. Following this assertion he goes on to state that religion is 'our truest comfort: for if already we are happy, it is a pleasure to think that we can make that happiness unending; and if we are miserable, it is very consoling to think that there is a place of rest'. And, 'Thus, to the fortunate, religion holds out a continuation of bliss; to the wretched, a change from pain'. In fact, as far as Primrose is concerned, the fortunate do rather less well than the wretched simply because, 'To the first, eternity is but a single blessing, since at most it but increases what they already possess. To the latter, it is a double advantage; for it diminishes their pain here, and rewards them with heavenly bliss hereafter'.[53] The wretched have the additional benefit – according to the Vicar – of suffering less than others when they actually die: 'for, after a certain degree of pain, every new breach that death opens in the constitution nature kindly covers with insensibility'. So those who are no strangers to hardship become insensitive to their own suffering. Primrose continues, 'Thus Providence has given the wretched two advantages over the happy in this life, – greater felicity in dying, and in heaven all that superiority of pleasure which arises from contrasted enjoyment'.[54]

From all this the Vicar concludes that 'religion does what philosophy could never do: it shows the equal dealings of Heaven to the happy and the unhappy, and levels all human enjoyments to nearly the same standard. It gives to both rich and poor the same happiness hereafter, and equal hopes to aspire after it; but if the rich have the advantage of enjoying pleasure here, the poor have the endless satisfaction of knowing what it once was to be miserable'.[55] This is simply a piece of rhetoric designed to play down inequality and injustice through sophistry. The Vicar's line trivialises the suffering of real human beings by implying that human life is unimportant. Rather than arguing for changes in the conditions structuring the lives of the poor, Primrose offers a dubious comfort dependent upon the promise of happiness in a purely hypothetical realm. At the same time, this account reassures the rich that the inequality which allows them to lead opulent lives while others endure harsh ones is perfectly all right. It is just the result of Providence and therefore God-ordained and inevitable; consequently the rich are under no obligation to seek to improve the lives of the wretched. The sermon which Goldsmith expresses through the Vicar is an apology for economic, political and social inequality – it encourages the acceptance of oppression and exploitation by the poor, and ignores (indeed denies) the possibility of changes being undertaken 'on earth' by human beings. It is a case for total passivity and wishful thinking for the victims of injustice; contemporary reviewers and commentators imagined that Goldsmith's tale would be a great comfort to those experiencing harsh lives. Yet, quite apart from the fact that most of the poor could not read, still less afford to buy a book or use circulating libraries, it is hard to see why any solace should be derived from the book by any other than the fortunate, for whom the Vicar's proselytising provides a feeble vindication. Those amongst the deprived who would be satisfied by transcendental promises in preference to practical changes would surely have been few and far between.

7
Richard Graves:
The Spiritual Quixote (1773)

There are many ways to undermine a set of beliefs and practices of which one does not approve; one may impute lunacy or roguery to one's opponents; one may suggest that the appeal of the offending beliefs is confined to social inferiors who are, by definition, ignorant; one may seek to demonstrate that the content of the alternative *Weltanschauung* is lacking in originality – a mere rehash of ideas long since refuted and condemned as worthless. Richard Graves, in *The Spiritual Quixote*, employed all of these techniques against Methodism; the author had himself been inconvenienced and humiliated by an itinerant preacher, and his younger brother had – to the horror of his family – been strongly influenced by the Wesleys. However, what concerns us here is Graves as a novelist and a minister of the Anglican Church; it is in this context that his view of Methodism becomes relevant.

For most of the novel the hero, Geoffry Wildgoose, is shown as a man suffering from mental disturbance. This is triggered by a secular argument with the local clergyman, Powell, and exacerbated when Wildgoose mistakenly supposes that one of Powell's subsequent sermons is directed against him in particular. To make matters worse Wildgoose finds some old radical-Protestant literature and, 'this *crude trash* happened to suit Mr. Geoffry's vitiated palate: especially as these writings abounded with bitter invectives against the regular clergy, and the established church'. The various pamphlets which Wildgoose finds may represent different sects, but they all display 'inveteracy against the Church of England'. Graves makes it plain that this material is rubbish written by those with an absurd hatred for Anglicanism; moreover, it is obsolete rubbish. Nevertheless, 'This was no unpleasant food for Wildgoose's *disorder*. For, having conceived so great a prejudice against the vicar of the parish, he gladly embraced any system, that seemed to thwart his usual doctrine'.[1]

The effect of the 'Puritanical principles' which Wildgoose absorbs from the old tracts is a susceptibility to Methodist doctrines; consequently, he is afflicted by 'that sort of phrenzy, which we ascribe to enthusiasts in music, poetry, or painting; or in any other art or science; *whose imaginations are so entirely possessed by those ideas, as to make them talk and act like madmen, in the sober eyes of merely rational people'.*[2] At this point 'some straggling itinerant' arrives and Wildgoose's madness is consolidated – as demonstrated by the fact that he begins to frequent the socially-inferior Jerry Tugwell's home, along with 'labourers and mechanics'. These working-class men are interested in Methodism, but Wildgoose is atypical, suggests Graves, precisely because 'people in high life are less prone to that excess of zeal or religious enthusiasm'. Jerry, who later becomes the hero's companion in absurdity, already has the reputation of being a half-wit, given his lack of 'prudence'.[3]

Wildgoose soon begins to test his own oratorical skills upon his companions who, 'though they were not capable of distinguishing nicely between his doctrine and what they heard at church; yet being delivered to them in a more familiar manner, and by a new teacher, and in a new place, it made a considerable impression'.[4] It is novelty of presentation which attracts these illiterate workers to the hero's harangues – they are quite ignorant of any intellectual content which his sermonising might contain; in this, implies Graves, they are no different from all of the other plebeians who listen to Methodist preaching. As Wildgoose reaches the emotional pitch of his performance he foams at the mouth and confesses to 'crimes'; these are, of course, metaphorical crimes, much to the confusion of his untutored listeners. For Graves, Wildgoose's condition is the result of his having spent so long brooding over Puritan and Methodist tracts (Graves makes little distinction between the two); their 'strange jargon', 'chiefly consists in applying quaint Hebraisms of the Old Testament and the peculiar expressions of the primitive apostles to their own situations, and every trifling occurrence of modern life'.[5] Methodism is not even unique enough to constitute a sect, according to Graves, and the only innovation it champions is illegal: 'I know of few novel opinions which they maintain, except that of the lawfulness of preaching without a legal call; and of assembling in conventicles or in the open fields in direct opposition to the laws of the land'.[6]

The theme of madness runs throughout the novel; when Powell learns that the hero has left home to spread the gospel he remarks, 'there is no reasoning with people who refer you to their own inward feelings; which you can no more deny than they can prove: and who take for sacred the wildest suggestions of their own fancy'.[7] True, but Graves certainly wants to deny the validity of Wildgoose's interpretation of such feelings, so that they can be labelled 'wild', the product of 'fancy'. Wildgoose is so far gone that he fails to respond to Powell's letter informing him of his own mother's distress, for, 'Enthusiasm is deaf to the calls of Nature; nay, it esteems it meritorious to trample upon all the relative duties of life. Men of this cast think nothing of any importance, but what corresponds with the *chimerical notions which have possessed their fancies'*.[8] As Mr Rivers finds when he tries to talk 'sense' to Wildgoose, 'reasoning with a man under the influence of any passion is like endeavouring to stop a wild horse, who becomes more violent from being pursued'.[9]

Graves takes the lunatic nature of his hero's enterprise to its logical conclusion at one of Wildgoose's meetings: a local madman (allegedly driven insane by Wesley's preaching) turns up and bawls out a stream of incomprehensible nonsense. The local people know the man to be deranged but Wildgoose, in his stupidity, assumes that the man's behaviour is a proof of *holiness*. The author's point is clear: enthusiasts, such as the Methodists, simply cannot (or will not) recognise the difference between 'grace' and plain mental illness. Eventually even Jerry comes to think that Wildgoose is 'crackbrained', but it is not until the hero is rendered unconscious by a missile that he himself begins to doubt his calling.[10] Luckily for Wildgoose he is cared for by Greville, an Anglican paragon, who is prepared to try to counteract the workings of Wildgoose's 'deluded imagination'.[11]

Greville's efforts, plus the blow on the head and the prospect of marrying Julia Townsend, lead to Wildgoose's return to sanity, which in this case means religious and political orthodoxy. The hero's lunacy has therefore been transitory, largely a consequence of his vanity and his flouting of social conventions; in essence, acting in a manner inappropriate to his social standing. For Graves, Methodism only appeals to people of low rank and little or no education and – occasionally – members of the upper or middle classes *if they are particularly stupid or mentally disturbed*. It is unthinkable that any well-educated person of rank could be seriously attracted to any form of enthusiasm for long; that is why the hero of this novel is mentally deranged for the greater part of the work, even though he displays moments of lucidity in order to convey Graves's own opinions to the reader – as demonstrated by Wildgoose's conversation with Mrs Booby.[12]

So much for the mad; Jerry is a prime example of Methodism's appeal to the ignorant; he quickly absorbs scraps of Wildgoose's rhetoric and is exceedingly deferential to any opinion which he supposes to stem from a reading of the Bible, even if it involves scripture being 'absurdly applied', as it frequently is by his master.[13] To remind us that Jerry is an idiot Graves introduces a variety of ludicrous incidents, such as the one where Tugwell mistakes a jack-ass for a stag; one feels that Graves subscribes to the view of Mr Pottle, who deems the lower classes to be gullible yet conniving 'bumpkins'.[14]

The inability of Wildgoose's listeners to understand what he is talking about is demonstrated throughout, his speech to a keeper and his wife being just one example of the fact that 'Wildgoose did not reflect upon the improbability of his audience's not compre-hending his allegorical meaning'.[15] Graves had no such illusions regarding the understanding of working people, as he shows in his comments on the use of calling cards, his main point being that social inferiors blindly follow conventions which they do not under-stand: it does not occur to him that such blind imitation could be cited as a partial explanation for such plebeian attachment as there was to the Anglican Church.[16] Perhaps the most risible instance of working-class ignorance occurs when Wildgoose preaches to a Welsh crowd who give him a very favourable reception, notwithstanding the fact that at least half of them cannot understand English.[17] So, upper-class lunacy and working-class illiteracy both find expression in Methodism, such handicaps being – according to Graves – a precondition for the emergence of the Methodist movement and the means by which it flourished.

As noted above, one of Graves's major criticisms of the Method-ists was that they were fighting battles long since won; it is in this sense that he saw the activities of enthusiasts as quixotism. 'Primi-tive reformers' had good cause to act as they did and were inspired by the 'Holy Spirit' to perform specific tasks:

But our modern itinerant reformers, *by the mere force of imagination,* have conjured up the powers of darkness in an enlightened age. *They are acting in defiance of human laws, without any apparent neces-sity, or any divine commission.* They are planting the gospel in a Christian country: they are combating the shadow of Popery, where the Protestant religion is established; and declaiming against good works, in an age which they usually represent as abounding in every evil work.[18]

Here Graves is asserting, but not proving, that the Methodists are not divinely inspired and that there is no need for their work, Protestantism being secure; he is also misrepresenting their position by implying that their attack on 'good works' involves a comparison of good with evil works and not – as the Methodists were wont to argue – a conflict between the doctrine of good works as opposed to 'justification by faith'. As for the view that evangelical activity was once essential but no longer valid, the fact is that many eighteenth-century Christians (including some Anglicans) did not share Graves's view. We now know that the complacency which characterised a large part of the Anglican clergy was both unwarranted and very damaging to the Established Church. As Gilbert observes: 'The period 1740–1830 was an era of disaster, for whereas the Church of England had controlled something approaching a monopoly of English religious practice only ninety years earlier, in 1830 it was on the point of becoming a minority religious Establishment'.[19]

As if to sweeten the pill Graves uses the character of Mr Graham to present his criticism in a modified form; Mr Graham finds the idea of itineracy quite attractive and rejects the view that religion should be dependent upon a few minor points. He goes on argue:

> I really believe, when the Methodists first set out (as Providence often brings about salutary ends by irregular means) they did some good, and contributed to rouse the negligent clergy, and to revive practical Christianity amongst us. But, I am afraid, *they have since done no small prejudice to Religion, by reviving cobweb disputes of the last century; and by calling off the minds of men from practice, to mere speculation.*[20]

Again, the charge is that Methodism raises obsolete and trivial issues; to pat the Methodists on the back for their contribution towards the revival of 'practical Christianity' is simply tendentious: by this term Anglicans meant good works, the very doctrine which Methodists (Calvinist or Arminian) consistently opposed. Additionally, the claim that they encouraged speculation as against activism is unjustifiable – but the mode of activity which they valued was evangelical rather than philanthropic.[21] The way in which Graves

employs the character Graham here, has led a number of commentators to overestimate the author's own amiability and to attribute to
him a conciliatory and flexible attitude towards Methodism.

Graves's sympathetic treatment of Anglican ministers is illustrated by the characters of Gregory Griskin and Dr Greville. The
most important thing about Griskin seems to be the fact that his
relationship with his parishioners does not depart from protocol and
does not undermine class dominance; he is the sort of clergyman
who insists upon the payment of tithes even if he is often ready to
return that which has been given. In this way, suggests Graves, the
minister not only protects his 'rights' but also reinforces the social
distance between himself and his 'flock'.[22] As we shall see below,
Graves was most concerned that class and status distinctions should
remain secure. Greville is probably the most important clergyman in
the novel and Graves's initial description of this worthy allows him
to throw another sop to the Methodists: 'Dr. Greville was what Mr.
Wesley and his associates *ought to have been*, and what (I sincerely
believe) they at first intended to be'. But Graves must have known
that the Methodists had no intention whatever of being like the
fictitious Greville, for he 'had a *Faith*, which worked by *Love*; or, in
modern language, *his belief of the truths of the Gospel made him consider
as an indispensable duty those acts of beneficence which his humanity
prompted him to perform*'.[23] Once again Graves insists that the very
thing which Wesley et al. were determined to attack was that which
they really wanted to do; but this attempt to incorporate the Methodists just does not work.

Towards the end of the novel Greville sums up most of Graves's
objections to Methodism; on the charge that they violated law and
ignored protocol he states: 'we are commanded "to submit to every
ordinance of man, for *the Lord's* sake; to let everything be done
decently and in order:" and therefore no one has a right to break
through the regulations of society, merely from the suggestions of
his own fancy, unless he can give some visible proof of a supernatu-
ral commission'.[24] Greville concedes that 'there may be some cause
of complaint against the negligence of the Clergy; and that, if the
people had plenty of wholesome food or sound doctrine, they would
not be hankering after the cruder trash of *some* of your itinerant
Preachers. But does this warrant every ignorant Mechanic to take the
staff out of the hands of the Clergy, and set up for Reformers in
Religion?'.[25] However, Greville's admission of clerical failings is
purely formal and complacent, as is his solution: 'let application be

made to the Bishop of the diocese'.[26] The truth is that the bishops
were at least as guilty of laxity as the humbler functionaries of the
Established Church. Greville further wishes to claim that such success as the Methodists have enjoyed has not resulted from the religious content of their preaching:

> As to the particular doctrines which the Methodists *pretend to have
> revived*, and on which they lay so great a stress; I do not imagine,
> the advantage which they seem to have *gained* over the regular
> Clergy arises from those *cobweb distinctions*, which, I am con-
> vinced, *not one in ten of their followers really comprehend*: but from
> the seriousness of their lives, and the vehemence and earnestness
> of their harangues; which may have a temporary effect upon their
> audience whilst the impression on their fancy lasts; and have, I
> believe, really awakened many indolent and careless Christians to
> a sober and devout life.[27]

Up to this point Graves has consistently argued that the Methodists
have revived old doctrines and controversies; now he suggests that
they have only 'pretended' to do this. The controversial points upon
which the Methodists placed so much emphasis are brushed aside as
'cobweb distinctions' and their success is discounted as nothing
more than temporary emotionalism. In keeping with Graves's 'softly-
softly' approach Greville magnanimously observes that the Methodists may have inspired certain previously apathetic Christians, and it
is interesting that he recognises the 'seriousness' of the lives of some
leading Methodists. However we are soon back to the works/faith
issue with Greville claiming that the Methodists have misinterpreted
Anglicanism here; this is amusing given Graves's stubborn refusal to
understand Methodist doctrine.[28]

Graves hoped that Methodism would be defeated by its own
excesses; whilst he had fewer objections to educated, middle-class
preachers like Wesley, he maintained that their doctrines would
attract those who saw preaching as an easy alternative to 'the drudg-
ery of a mechanic trade'. Moreover he expected the consequences of
the respectable Methodists' sermonising to be largely negative: 'after
prejudicing the people against their proper Pastors, they will leave
them prey to the ignorance, and perhaps much greater immorality,
of illiterate Plebeians; and so will have made another schism in our
Church to very little purpose'.[29] Graves could probably imagine
nothing worse than that illiterate plebs might adopt the position of

religious functionaries; for him the purpose of the Church was to teach working people moral lessons, and keep them firmly in their place.

Recent commentators – whether sympathetic or hostile to Methodism – agree that John Wesley, the most influential of the Methodist leaders, was rigidly conservative in his political views. However they also perceive why Wesley's contemporaries thought that his flouting of Anglican authority and his conception of Christianity gave some encouragement to the rejection of established authority in general. As Cannon points out, 'It is in part because organised religion was expected to be a prop of the social order that the authorities were so suspicious of the Methodist movement . . . Old Dissent had shown what it could do as the driving force behind radical change in the seventeenth century and Methodism seemed at first to be heading in the same direction'.[30] As it turns out we now know that the Church of England was the only major institution to really suffer from the Methodist rejection; those eighteenth-century Anglican critics who predicted that any weakening of the Established Church would lead to complete chaos and anarchy may have overstated their case somewhat, but they understood the threat to the Church rather more clearly than some modern critics appreciate.

R. E. Davies, himself a Methodist minister, argues that mob violence against the Methodists was fostered by Anglican clergy and squires 'who thought that Wesley was giving the lower orders ideas above their station'; such hostility 'sometimes arose from the real but *entirely unfounded* conviction that Wesley was stirring up rebellion against proper authority'.[31] In fact this conviction was unequivocally founded upon Wesley's own behaviour towards 'proper authority', and the fact that he *did* encourage others to follow his example in flouting the authority of the Church. Davies's description of the controversy between Bishop Butler and Wesley indicates that he should recognise all this; as he states of Butler, 'he was right in thinking that Wesley's activities could not be contained within the Church of England as it then was; *they were subversive of diocesan and parochial discipline*'. As Davies further admits of Wesley's claim to rightfully continue preaching at Bristol, 'legally he was quite wrong'.[32] Once this is conceded all of the apologetics of 'divine call' and so on do not alter the fact that Wesley continually disobeyed (and incited others to disobey) what Anglicans deemed 'proper authority'.

A. Armstrong has recently written of Wesley, 'the threat he produced to church order and to the social order was either ignored or

not understood by him'.[33] Perhaps Wesley ignored the potential
disruptiveness of his own doctrines, but it is impossible to believe
that he was incapable of understanding how Methodism jeopard-
ised 'church order'. As Gilbert has pointed out in his discussion of
the Methodist societies:

> There was an obvious ambiguity in the claims of voluntary agen-
> cies to be subordinate to the authority of the parochial clergy.
> *Their very existence reflected both the partial breakdown of the organisa-*
> *tional machinery of the Church and the increasing erosion of the pre-*
> *scriptive powers of its ministers*, and they performed religious-cul-
> tural functions which the majority of the parochial clergy were
> capable of performing inadequately, if at all.[34]

Pace Clark, the appearance of Methodism and Evangelicalism does
not so much indicate 'the intellectual vitality and strength of Orthodox churchmanship in the eighteenth century', but rather the steady
decline of Anglican dominance in religious matters.[35]

The bulk of Graves's objections to Methodism applied to both the
Calvinist and Arminian versions promoted by Whitefield and Wesley
respectively; it is true that Graves heaps derision on Whitefield in
the novel, and treats Wesley much more tenderly, but it must not be
supposed that Graves had a great deal of sympathy for the latter's
doctrines (Whitefield was a more likely target, being of lower social
status and – by all accounts – a more histrionic performer). T. B.
Shepherd has mistakenly assumed that because Graves does not
attack Wesley personally, then he must virtually support him; no
mention of the fact that one of the author's characters has been
driven mad by Wesley's teaching. Shepherd detects 'a constant note
of approval' for certain traits which Graves attributes to Methodists,
thereby failing to see beyond the author's patronising and incorpo-
rating view of the Methodist project.[36] Perhaps this is to be expected
given that Shepherd has earlier misrepresented the first few chapters of the novel by constructing a chronologically-distorted synop-
sis of the action.[37] He further claims that as Graves has made
Wildgoose one of 'good birth and education' – and thus a character
with whom one can have some 'sympathy' – this indicates the author's own fraternal feelings for the Methodists.[38] In all this Shepherd is mistaken; his study portrays Graves as a closet-enthusiast
and Smollett as one who 'might well be an advocate for the need of
methodism or some such movement in England'.[39] No matter that

both writers saw Methodism as the prerogative of the insane and the ignorant: a religion for upper-class lunatics, bourgeois 'old maids', and illiterate workers. The fact is that, as C. J. Hill has noted, *The Spiritual Quixote* 'is first of all the literary monument of anti-Methodism'.[40]

Graves's female characters are somewhat more varied than those of most other eighteenth-century prose-fiction writers; whilst he does employ paragons (of whom there are three) and 'wicked' women, he does not confine himself to these categories and thus enhances the plausibility of even his minor female characters. Mrs Sarsenet and Miss Sainthill are good examples of how Graves manages to suggest greater complexity of character than might be expected from such brief sketches, and Julia Townsend – the heroine – is all the more believable for being imperfect and appearing infrequently throughout the story.[41] Julia is no beauty, and is far from deferential to Wildgoose, whose religious views she openly mocks; whilst she reprimands *him* for having abandoned his mother, she herself has run away from home, albeit for the immediately practical reason of bad treatment at the hands of her family. In spite of her youth (she is about sixteen according to Wildgoose's estimate) Julia is resourceful and has already managed to escape 'ruin' whilst lodging at the house of a procuress in London.[42]

In eighteenth-century novels, running away from home is usually confined to vain and stupid young women, but Julia is quite level-headed; indeed, her interest in Wildgoose is based upon the solid attractions of his looks and his fortune. Graves explains:

I would not insinuate that Miss Townsend was of a mercenary temper (for she really was not). But though fortune alone, where the person is disagreeable, has seldom any considerable influence over the affections of a young girl: yet, I believe, in conjunction with other circumstances, it operates insensibly upon their fancies, and contributes to make the person possessed of it more agreeable than he would otherwise appear; as the want of fortune frequently prevents their seeing those perfections in a man, which he is really possessed of.[43]

Additionally, Julia is susceptible to an emotion rarely found among literary heroines of the period: jealousy. When Wildgoose preaches at Bristol he becomes very popular with the female Methodists, one of whom is 'leering over his shoulder' as Julia watches from the audience. The heroine promptly faints, or, as Graves puts it, 'was fallen into an hysteric fit'; the author observes that as Julia was 'fatigued with her journey, and perhaps somewhat affected at the sight of Mr. Wildgoose's gallantry to Mrs. Culpepper, it was more than her delicate constitution could well support'.[44] If further proof were required to establish the cause of Julia's swoon it appears when she, Mrs Sarsenet, and Wildgoose go to hear Whitefield preach; Julia does not want to go at all, but when she finally does she 'absolutely refused to go into the desk (whither she was invited), because she saw the same Mrs. Culpepper there, whom she had seen him gallanting out of the desk the night before at the Tabernacle'.[45]

In itself fainting through jealousy may appear trivial or simply comical, but it is noteworthy that Graves's use of the fainting device differs from its usual application. As Needham and Utter have argued, fainting occurs throughout English literature, but in the eighteenth century it is typically associated with romantic heroines who faint at any sign of sexual intention on the part of male characters. There was an altruistic alternative to self-protective fainting, as manifested by Henry Fielding's Sophia Western – who faints when others are harmed or in danger; whilst Julia is subject to altruistic fainting on one occasion, she is singular as a heroine who faints from jealousy.[46]

The distance between Julia and the more typical eighteenth-century heroine becomes clear if we compare her with one of Graves's minor characters, Charlotte Rivers, who – in certain respects – epitomises the literary paradigm for female virtue popular during the period.[47] Charlotte *'had so striking an appearance, that few people could behold her without admiration'*. In keeping with her humble origins she is healthy rather than perilously delicate; although the eighteenth-century heroine was not expected to be too robust, various novelists (including Goldsmith, Henry Fielding, and Burney) took some pains to reject the equation of physical weakness with femininity. Predictably Charlotte has 'good nature and good sense', 'virgin innocence', and 'native modesty' among many other fine qualities, and one might assume that this left little else to be desired.[48] However, this is not enough for Mr Rivers, so Charlotte is obliged to spend some time in London in order to become more refined and fashionable.[49]

When she returns home she is 'greatly improved . . . both in her carriage, her manner, and in the delicacy of her complexion'. So much so that 'The fame of Mrs. Rivers' beauty and appearance soon spread amongst the neighbouring villages'. Nevertheless this does not prevent her from becoming a perfect wife and mother; Wildgoose notes that she looks upon her son 'with inexpressible sweetness, and the air of a Madonna by Raphael or Corregio', and Rivers tells him, 'it is incredible, with Mrs. Rivers' oeconomy, how small an income supplies us plentifully with all the elegancies which temperance and an unexpensive taste require'.[50] Charlotte's story illustrates the basic plot for a number of eighteenth-century novels: a beautiful, virtuous, low-status girl is courted by a man who is her social superior; having overcome many vicissitudes (often including the prejudice of the man's friends and relatives), the couple marry and the 'fair nymph' becomes an unparalleled wife and mother who devotes her life to her family and to the local paupers.

As noted above, Julia is neither beautiful nor deferential; however, her family background is at least as distinguished as that of Wildgoose, so she apparently does not need the remedial training in 'feminine accomplishments' which Charlotte undergoes. Graves makes no mention of Julia subsequently having any children, nor does he comment on her skill regarding household economy; perhaps this is because the marriage between her and Wildgoose is one between social equals (and therefore cannot be considered 'imprudent'), so she does not need to display any special qualities by which the match can be vindicated.[51]

Some insight into Graves's attitude towards women can be gleaned from the conversation between Wildgoose and Mrs Booby; the hero almost certainly expresses Graves's opinions here as Mrs Booby's ideas are discredited along with her motives for speaking to Wildgoose.[52] She presents herself to him as 'A Lady who is disgusted with the world', but her desire to see him rests – at least in part – on his 'agreeable countenance'. Mrs Booby tells Wildgoose that she has left her husband after three years of loveless marriage, and lists her spouse's faults to justify her action. Mr Booby is described as slovenly, preoccupied with hunting and drinking, dismissive of 'genteel company', and convinced of 'the authority of the husband over us poor domestic animals, called wives'.[53]

Her ostensible purpose in telling Wildgoose her story is to discover 'whether I have done anything inconsistent with my marriage vow'; the question amazes the hero almost as much as the fact that she has left her husband in the first place. However, he points out that as the marriage was not based upon 'mutual affection' or 'religious principle' it is not surprising that it has been unhappy, adding: 'you have not sufficiently considered your obligation to *obey* the person, to whom you have, by the marriage-contract, given up, in some measure, your natural freedom'. Mrs Booby replies that she would rather give up her life, but Wildgoose proceeds to argue that such an obligation is 'evidently enjoined by the Holy Scripture, *and to be deduced from that superiority which Nature seems to have given the man over the more delicate sex'*.[54] Mrs Booby rejects this claim of male superiority, so Wildgoose – sidestepping the issue of inequality between the sexes – states that domestic government, like civil government, requires a *'sovereign* power': 'And I am certain that Religion, as well as Reason, has placed this power in the husband'. Mrs Booby will have none of this, but Wildgoose persists, speculating that if she had submitted to her husband and 'acknowledged her entire dependence upon him for support and protection' then she would have been considerably happier. The reasoning behind this is that if a woman presents herself as a 'poor and helpless creature' rather than 'displaying that *masculine* ferocity which is too common in the sex', then no man could be so 'brutish' as to treat her badly.[55]

The lady has nothing but contempt for this particular option and informs Wildgoose that her pin-money makes her perfectly capable of looking after herself; for the hero pin-money is 'monstrous':

> The allowing a woman a maintenance, independent of her husband, is not only destroying that mutual affection which arises from a sense of their interest being inseparably united; but it is also a continual temptation to a woman to fly out on the slightest dispute: and to despise the authority of an husband without whose assistance or support she has it in her power to live in affluence and splendor.[56]

But Wildgoose's remarks are clearly inappropriate in this case – pin-money has not destroyed mutual affection for none was ever present. What it did undermine was not mutual affection or the consciousness of joint interest, but rather the authority of the husband insofar as it was based upon his economic position. The need for helplessness and submissiveness on the part of wives disappears when a married woman has sufficient economic independence to challenge her husband's economic domination. For Graves the idea of women being in any way independent was undoubtedly an unpalatable one.

Before Wildgoose leaves Mrs Booby to pursue his mission we learn that she is fully engaged in the frivolities she affects to despise, and that her disgust for the world arises from a bad run at cards and the fact that her former lover, Clayton, has arrived at Bath with his new wife, 'a very agreeable heiress with thirty thousand pounds'; adding insult to injury, he has held a public breakfast to which Mrs Booby has not been invited.[57] Thus the lady is discredited.

The general attitude which Graves expresses towards the social hierarchy in his novel is that distinctions necessarily exist and must be carefully maintained. He definitely viewed the 'lower orders' with some contempt as is illustrated by his frequent comments on their ignorance and credulity; however, he was both amused and irritated by the way in which individuals from one particular class or strata sometimes attempt to 'pass' as members of another group.[58] Wildgoose's appearance belies his gentry origins and leads Whitefield's sister to term him and Jerry 'trampers': 'And although Wildgoose had of late affected to despise all worldly distinctions, and to make light of external respect, the consequence of them; yet he was a little shocked at this unforeseen effect of his voluntary humiliation, and almost began to wish that he had travelled in a manner more suited to his station in life'.[59] For Graves, any member of the 'respectable' classes who is stupid enough to conceal or disregard his or her status deserves to suffer the – probably unpleasant – consequences (the treatment Wildgoose receives from Mrs Booby's footman is a good example).

The concealment of class identity occurs several times in the novel, and if Wildgoose's passing involves demeaning himself, the passing affected by Rouvell, a one-time servitor from Wildgoose's Oxford college, allows him to mix freely with his social superiors.[60] The hero tries to persuade Rouvell that education and behaviour are the most important (and equalising) aspects of being a gentleman, and that whilst there is nothing wrong with humble origins, seeking to conceal such origins is ridiculous. Rouvell believes that the advantages of mixing with 'people of distinction' justify chicanery, and confides that he is thinking of taking orders to secure a good living, even though he has little concern for religion.[61] The last we hear of this character is that – having failed in his bid to marry a wealthy woman – he has married modestly and is about to enter the Anglican Church. His motivation for becoming a clergyman remains financial, so he ceases to pass as person of fashion only to pose as a man of religion.[62] In either role he is an impostor, and for Graves such people insidiously undermine existing social relations and institutions.

Although Graves tells the reader that Wildgoose has tried to ignore social distinctions during his itineracy, there is little evidence of this in the text. Whenever he and Tugwell are invited into a respectable home Jerry invariably ends up in the kitchen.[63] And when Jerry becomes annoyed at the attitude of a couple of locals as he and Wildgoose enter Bath, the hero informs him that 'the *mob* of all places were alike; and that he ought not to reflect upon a whole body of people, for the wanton petulance of a few ignorant wretches'.[64] Yet by employing the term 'mob' Wildgoose is doing much the same thing – particularly as the basis for his comments is simply that a 'taylor's 'prentice' has made an irreverent remark to them and an elderly man has (accidentally or otherwise) given them ambiguous directions. 'Mob' was an ideological category employed by the ruling and middle classes to refer to ordinary working people, especially, but not only, when the latter sought to influence events by mass protest and so on. Essentially the term was used to designate all of those common people over whom the 'respectable' classes had no immediate control; Wildgoose's usage does not differ from that of his non-Methodist social equals, and would include Jerry were it not that the latter is his servant.

When Jerry and Wildgoose pass some forgeworkers on the road Tugwell observes, 'how hard it [is] that some people should be forced to toil like slaves, whilst others [live] in ease and plenty, and the fat of the land!'. Wildgoose argues that true happiness resides in religious rather than material circumstances, that 'there is not that difference in the real enjoyment of men, that you imagine', and that Tugwell knows nothing of the cares which plague the rich and are harder to bear 'than any bodily labour which poor people undergo'. Jerry is rightly sceptical about this proposition and replies that if he had a really good dinner every day he would not trouble himself with cares and anxieties. Wildgoose's weak reply is that 'these distinctions amongst mankind are absolutely necessary; and whilst men have the liberty of doing as they please, it cannot be otherwise'. Jerry remains unconvinced, stating, 'methinks it is very hard, that one man should have five or six hundred pounds a-year, when another mayhap has not fifty'.[65] The hero then introduces the idea that if everyone had £100 per annum nobody would work for another, but would have to make for themselves any and every thing which they required. And this, according to Wildgoose, means that 'either every man must work ten times harder than the poorest man now does, or, if he were idle or extravagant, those that were frugal and industrious would *again* grow rich, and the others poor: which shows the unavoidable necessity of that inequality amongst mankind, with which your complaint began'.[66] Jerry is stumped at this point, but whilst such arguments might confuse an uneducated artisan, they do not amount to much.

Wildgoose's claim that happiness consists of religious conviction and experience is quite irrelevant to Jerry's contention that some work like slaves whilst others live in ease. As Wildgoose nowhere expresses the opinion that one cannot be both materially comfortable and spiritually secure, he should be able to consider material comfort quite apart from religion. The claim that the wealthy only *appear* to enjoy themselves whilst suffering more than manual workers suggests that labourers have no worries of their own; the idea is that the rich have luxury marred by anxiety whereas the poor have labour but not a care in the world. In fact the rich had luxury and may or may not have had worries; the poor had no luxury, plenty of hard physical work if employed, and an adequate portion of worries. It is therefore easy to see which group had the greatest opportunity for 'real enjoyment'. In the eighteenth century it was often suggested that the poor – like animals – had no cares, but it is hard to believe that an educated man like Graves really thought that the trials of the affluent were comparable to those experienced by the poor. Stripped of rhetoric the attitude voiced by the hero is one of indifference to the suffering of the poor.

The notion that social distinctions are inevitable because 'men have the liberty of doing as they please' makes little sense, for it must have been patently obvious that most men and women were in no position to do as they pleased; only a tiny élite enjoyed this privilege. But the spurious reference to free choice has been introduced to imply that affluence and poverty occur because individuals possess different moral qualities, as is revealed in Wildgoose's comments on the hypothetical sharing-out of money. Surely the forgeworkers did not *choose* to toil like slaves; it is clear to Jerry that they are 'forced' to do such work in order to live. But accepting the ridiculous premise that these workers chose to perform unpleasant and arduous labour, why should they – having received their hypothetical £100 per annum – decide that they no longer wanted to work for another? Perhaps they had previously worked solely to procure the means to survive. Any human being who could choose exactly what he or she wanted to do would have no need of income, whether large or small, so it is clear that Wildgoose has employed a purely formal notion of choice in his rhetoric. The freedom of choice available to most of the population in eighteenth-century England was nothing other than the choice associated with formally-free wage-labour; this meant that when work was plentiful they could choose to work (and live with few comforts) or choose to starve. In practical terms this is no choice at all.

Wildgoose's redistribution-of-money scheme is posed within a totally ideological framework, being based upon the bourgeois economic assumption that every 'man' is an island; the implication is that (both in Wildgoose's example and in the existing society) there is no need for collective activities, just the bustle of individual producer-consumers. In this model, all activity takes place in a vacuum as everyone pursues their rational self-interest; but in contrast to this paradigm, 'Society does not consist of individuals; it expresses the sum of connections and relationships in which individuals find themselves'.[67] In short, economic models of this kind hypothesise conditions never yet seen in any human society.

Of course Wildgoose soon abandons the idea that no one would work for another in his imaginary world, for he goes on to argue that the 'frugal and industrious' would soon grow rich in such circumstances – by working for those who would not perform *their own tasks*. How this would be possible given that everyone had to work harder than ten men just to survive, is not made clear. What is obvious is that Wildgoose is surreptitiously arguing that those who are wealthy in the real world have become so by industry and thrift, hence the view that these worthies would – under Wildgoose's scheme – soon retrieve their wealth. Thus Wildgoose offers the bourgeois theory of primitive accumulation under the guise of necessity, conveniently ignoring the fact that – back in the real world – there has never been an initially-equal distribution of resources; the rich are rich, in bourgeois mythology, because they have worked hard, saved, and used their superior brains. The real story of this accumulation is somewhat different, for, as Marx notes, 'In actual history it is notorious that conquest, enslavement, robbery, murder, briefly force, play the greater part'.[68]

Predictably Graves was very concerned about the way in which Methodism might disrupt work, and he portrays a variety of labourers abandoning their tasks to listen to Methodist preaching.[69] Religion may be important, but for Graves it must not be allowed to interfere with secular economic tasks. Both Lady Forester and Miss Sainthill share this concern that work must remain inviolate; they support the establishment of Protestant nunneries but would not have them open to 'young women who might be useful in the world, as servants, milliners, or mantua-makers, and other necessary employments'. The nunneries which they envisage would simply be 'a refuge for young ladies of good families and small fortunes'.[70]

In Graves's opinion the labouring poor should pay attention to their work and enjoy it – like the servants of Sir William and Lady Forester, and the happy farm-labourers employed by Isabella and her husband.[71] The non-labouring poor (that is the old and infirm, and the unemployed) should be grateful for whatever their superiors choose to give them, unlike the recipients of Lady Forester's charity.[72] The Reverend Dr Greville – who often visits the 'poor and ignorant part of his parish' – has something to say about both the poor and rank generally, as we shall see below.

When Wildgoose and Greville encounter a young beggar on the road the clergyman gives him sixpence, telling Wildgoose that, 'although he did not like to encourage common beggars, he generally gave them some little matter to relieve their present distress: but not without a sharp reproof to those who appeared to be habituated to that idle practice'. This leads the pair to discuss the conditions necessary for an overall 'reformation' of the behaviour of the masses,

> with Greville arguing that neither the preaching of the Clergy, nor even the many penal laws, which were daily multiplied, would avail any thing towards the end proposed, unless some alteration could be produced in the manners of the people, by the influence of their superiors: the luxury and extravagance of the great and people in high life descends, as a fashion, amongst the crowd, and has infected every rank of people.[73]

Greville obviously believes that any improvement in his society must depend upon – and largely consist of – changes amongst the working people which have been engineered by their superiors. It is an indication of Greville's (and Graves's) élitist opinion of ordinary people that their very faults are assumed to arise from misguided and ludicrous attempts to ape their 'betters'. Indeed, Greville's proposed solution to social ills is based on the view that these mindless, pliable imitators can be led towards 'acceptable' behaviour regardless of their socio-economic circumstances. His limited criticism of the nobility and the monarchy rests entirely on the premise that their bad example encourages indolence and extravagance amongst the lower ranks, whilst their pampering of servants threatens to corrupt the bourgeoisie. So, rural workers should be confined to the poverty from which they so often tried to escape, in order that they might constitute a sizeable (and probably surplus) workforce for agricultural and handicraft production.

What Greville fails to recognise is that preaching and harsh penal laws are likely to have little effect upon people who are frequently forced to act contrary to both to ensure their survival. The flight from the countryside which he so deplores was itself an example of workers seeking new opportunities in the face of the development of capitalist agriculture; this unquestionably worsened the condition of subsistence farmers and agricultural labourers, encouraging them (and sometimes forcing them) to search for a livelihood elsewhere. However, the underlying concern of Greville's speech is the same as that of every other character in the novel who speaks in favour of social distinctions and against Methodism: in this way Wildgoose (in his lucid moments), Rivers, Griskin et al. all voice Graves's opinions. For the author the issue is social order; as C. J. Hill writes of Graves: 'Every reflection, direct or indirect, of his political and religious faith shows him to have been a complete status-quo-ite, entirely satisfied with existing institution, and sincerely disturbed by anything which seemed to endanger them'.[74] Graves's desire to support existing social relations provides him with the basic theme of his novel, and although it must be said that the work is most amusing and enjoyable it was not intended to be a mere entertainment.

Since Hill's sound work, assessments of *The Spiritual Quixote* have typically ignored or overlooked the purpose of the book. Whibley saw the novel as a 'comedy of manners', and Graves as a 'wise patriot'; an anonymous reviewer in the TLS claimed that Graves was an advocate of 'robust common sense', whilst the editor of the 'Oxford English Novels' edition of the work repeats the idea of Graves's 'common sense' and concludes that Graves's views were 'moderate and conciliatory'.[75] Rymer, who maintains that Graves was definitely mounting a satirical attack on Methodism, has consequently argued that: 'On the whole, Graves has been idealized and treated with a sentimentality which, judging by his characteristic irony of tone and self-deprecating humour, he would probably have resented'.[76] One does not have to agree with all of Rymer's further contentions about the novel to concede this much. The most extensive commentary upon Graves's life, writings, and social views remains that of C. J. Hill, who describes the author as 'wholly mistrustful of democratic ideals' and 'the levelling principle'; a 'wholehearted believer in rank and form' who 'had a profound reverence for tradition and an obsequious respect for rank'.[77] As Hill concludes, 'Graves feared intellectual anarchy, revolution, and irreligion, and one, he thought, would be pretty sure to breed the others'.[78] This conclusion can, I suggest, be supported with reference to some of those features discussed in this chapter, for Graves was a man who, like Greville, 'would not have truth propagated in a seditious manner'.[79]

8
Fanny Burney:
Evelina (1778)

One noticeable feature of Fanny Burney's *Evelina* is that it presents the reader with characters whose differing views regarding women can be placed into three distinct groupings: (1) the genteel or polite mode; (2) the misogynistic or 'masculine' mode; (3) the instrumental-sexual mode. These perspectives are not mutually exclusive, to the extent that statements derived from the genteel mode may be tendentiously employed by those who basically subscribe to the instrumental mode and so on. Burney's approach involves comparing these three perspectives and indicating to the reader her full support for the first of them. At no point in the novel does she criticise this particular mode, which is accepted and propounded as being morally, practically and aesthetically correct; in contrast, modes (2) and (3) are discredited by Evelina, and those who share her outlook, whenever they appear. How do these forms differ?

Evelina herself represents the female virtues valued by adherents to the genteel mode, and in keeping with other literary heroines of the period, is 'innocent as an angel, and artless as purity itself'. This opinion expressed by her guardian, Villars, is shared by Lady Howard who states: 'She is a little angel!' and, 'Her face and person answer my most refined ideas of complete beauty'.[1] All agree that in Evelina's case beauty is enhanced by good sense and not tied to folly, as Lady Howard suggests it frequently is. In addition Evelina has a strong sense of duty and obedience and, with Villars's encouragement, this even extends to complying with her grandmother, Madame Duval, who is a stupid and discreditable woman. In this as in everything else Villars reiterates the importance of 'prudence' – for women in general and Evelina in particular.

Lord Orville, the genteel hero of the novel, holds views which mesh neatly into those of the aforementioned characters. He is apt to consider (at least some) women as 'goddesses' and likewise to refer to 'the general sweetness of the sex'.[2] In contrast Lord Merton, the standard 'bad' aristocrat of the story, perceives women as objects of sexual pleasure and little else; he occasionally employs rhetoric about 'heavenly living objects' and so on but his fundamental attitude towards women represents the instrumental-sexual view.[3] Sexual innuendo and lust are characteristic of this stance; in its mild form it appears in the following remark which he makes to a young female companion: 'how can one sit by you, and be good? . . . when only to look at you is enough to make one wicked – or wish to be so?'. And, more typically, 'I don't know what the devil a woman lives for after thirty: she is only in other folks way'.[4] Merton is not alone in his view of women, as Sir Clement and Lovel have similar attitudes – even though Sir Clement takes care to express himself in a version of the polite mode; his general courtesy is, however, a matter of form, a means to an end.

All of the dubious characters associated with form (3) abhor physical and/or intellectual ability in women, as can be seen from the following: Lord Merton to Lady Louisa, 'your ladyship is merely delicate, – and devil take me if I ever had the least passion for an Amazon'. Coverley (whose position is, like that of Lovel, only hinted at) states 'I'd as soon see a woman chop wood, as hear her chop logic'. And Lovel informs the company that he has 'an insuperable aversion to strength, either of body or mind, in a female'. Perhaps Merton's final comment in this discussion best illustrates the position of those who endorse (3): 'a woman wants nothing to recommend her but beauty and good nature; in everything else she is either impertinent or unnatural. For my part, deuce take me if I ever wish to hear a word of sense from a woman as long as I live!'[5]

Characters subscribing to the genteel mode, including Villars, Orville, Howard, Mrs Mirvan et al., consider health – but not robustness – and intelligence to be desirable qualities for women. According to Villars, Evelina is a 'rustic' or, as she herself puts it, 'unpolished', but this arises from her 'innocence', a sheltered upbringing, and lack of familiarity with urban society; it does not indicate any lack of intelligence.[6] As Lord Orville suggests, 'credulity is the sister of innocence'; he goes on to say that Evelina has 'an artlessness of disposition that I never saw equalled'. Nevertheless some measure of intellectual and moral independence is (arguably) attributed to women by the above characters and even Villars tells Evelina, 'you must learn not only to *judge* but to *act* for yourself'.[7]

The misogynistic view of women noted above centres around their various 'faults' as seen by the likes of Captain Mirvan and Tom

Branghton. The Captain believes that women, particularly young ones, are vacuous; speaking of Evelina and his daughter (who is not allowed to express her own opinions freely), he claims that 'they are a set of parrots and speak by rote, for they all say the same thing: but ask 'em how they like making puddings and pies, and I'll warrant you'll pose 'em'.[8] In response to remarks upon 'complexion' made by Orville and others, the Captain interjects, 'the women are vain enough already, no need for to puff 'em up more', and, displaying his contempt for the flattery lavished upon the two girls by syco- phants representing (3), he bluntly replies: 'I think you might as well not give the girls so much of this palaver: they'll take it all for gospel'. It must be noted however that Captain Mirvan is equally scornful of, yet amused by, pretensions amongst 'fashionable' men, and is unimpressed by polite society generally: 'the men, as they call themselves, are no better than monkeys; and as to the women, why they are mere dolls'.[9] So Mirvan is very much the spokesman for rough and impolite – but not sexually-oriented – 'male' values; there is nothing of the sycophant or the lover displayed in his character. The main objection which his wife, daughter and Evelina have concerning him is his outspoken and boisterous manner and his tendency to debunk, which in practice often amounts to physical cruelty. The practical jokes which he plays upon Mme Duval amply illustrate this trait: in turn he attacks her with smelling salts, con- trives to have her soused in mud, and ill-treats and terrorises her with a fake robbery. Given this, he incurs the disapproval of Villars and the others associated with model (1), although the clergyman cannot help sympathising with the Captain's attitude towards Lon- don and the fashionable. However, he is just too insensitive and impolite for the genteel; the sexually-motivated characters likewise find Mirvan uncultured and loutish, although this does not prevent Sir Clement from ingratiating himself with the Captain in order to gain access to Evelina.[10]

Two other characters who must be mentioned are the shabby- genteel Smith, and Tom Branghton. The former's stance is largely in keeping with (3), and a typical remark of this would-be ladies' man is, 'I always study what the ladies like, – that's my first thought. And, indeed, it is but natural that you should like best to sit by the gentlemen, for what can you find to say to one another?'. This prompts Tom to demonstrate his juvenile misogyny: 'O never think of that, they'll find enough to say, I'll be sworn. You know the women are never tired of talking'.[11]

Smith is extremely conceited – a trait encouraged by the high regard which Evelina's cousins have for him; he assumes that the heroine must find him attractive, and makes fawning statements like the following: 'how can you be so cruel as to be so much handsomer than your cousins?'. He is therefore horrified and hurt to find himself forced to dance solely with Mme Duval at a public ball to which he has escorted Evelina. Adopting what he sees as the last resort he speaks to the heroine of marriage which – in spite of the fact that he views it as resulting in 'loss of one's liberty' and the 'ridicule of all one's acquaintance' – he might be prepared to consider between himself and Evelina. His assumption is that marriage is the ultimate goal of all women, but in this he is stating no more than what is implicit in all of the perspectives on women mentioned above. His big mistake is to suppose that Evelina has any interest, romantic or otherwise, in *him*.[12]

Tom Branghton's approach is basically a rather more adolescent version of (2): he delights in being rude to his aunt, Mme Duval, finding her interest in dancing – given her age – particularly amusing. He likewise constantly endeavours to bait his sisters whom he claims are 'always scolding', and adds, 'there's nothing but quarreling with the women: it's my belief that they like it better than victuals and drink'. In keeping with his generally immature appraisal of the world, his overall attitude towards women leads him to perceive them as little more than suitable victims for his teasing and ignorant behaviour; like the Captain he shows no sign of any sexual interest in them.[13]

As noted earlier, Evelina is a paradigm of beauty, innocence and – in the main – good sense; in Lady Howard's words, 'She seems born for an ornament to the world'.[14] Almost everyone who comes into contact with her produces some cliché about her angelic or heavenly qualities; the use of such imagery by Orville, Lady Howard and Merton has already been noted but there are other examples such as when McCartney utters, 'Sweet Heaven! is this thy angel?', and Sir Clement refers to her as 'my angel'.[15] It is interesting to consider such terms as applied to women during this period for they are quite common in prose-fiction. The Puritan concern with godliness and grace has, one might argue, here been transformed into a secularised and trivial conception of goodness and divinity. Whilst the characters subscribing to (1) use divine imagery to refer to what they consider to be good behaviour and refined physical attractiveness, adherents to (3) equate words like 'angelic' and 'heavenly' simply with sexual desirability. In both cases the words have no religious meaning and in the former what is deemed good or morally correct is no more than behaviour which conforms to the bourgeois system of etiquette. By this I mean that the value system informing the genteel perspective is an ideological and formal position centring around discretion, prudence, circumspection and so on. This relates particularly to 'feminine delicacy', but expediency in all things is seen to constitute the highest virtue. What it is to be good is outlined below.

To be good is to be careful and restrained; it is to act according to the norms and values of bourgeois society in its most polished form, and thus be in harmony with the more 'noble' characteristics assumed to be present (if not always readily observable) within human nature. When Villars addresses Evelina on her stance towards McCartney he states, 'Though gentleness and modesty are the peculiar attributes of your sex, yet fortitude and firmness, when occasion demands them, are virtues as noble and becoming in women as in men: *the right line of conduct is the same for both sexes*, though the manner in which it is pursued, may somewhat vary, and be accommodated to the strength or weakness of the different travellers'.[16] So, regardless of different 'innate' traits, in certain circumstances it is both necessary and desirable for women to display what are essentially 'male' virtues (it may also be acceptable for men to possess a virtue associated with women, such as Lord Orville's 'feminine delicacy').[17] Villars's suggestion that there is one common standard for both sexes is, however, rather weakened by the equivocal qualification which he adds to it. And it is obvious that he does not – in practice – remain constant on this point. The idea of a common code here is used to combat female 'passivity' which is felt to be 'dangerous' on particular occasions. When Villars speaks to the heroine about Sir Clement's conduct it is clear what the clergyman has in mind: 'You cannot, my love, be too circumspect; the slightest carelessness on your part, will be taken advantage of, by a man of his disposition. It is not sufficient for you to be reserved; his conduct even calls for your resentment'. He goes on to advise, 'do not, by a too passive facility, risk the censure of the world, or your own future regret'.[18] Whilst passivity is generally considered to be a desirable female attribute then, it must not be maintained if reputation and honour (that is, virginity) are at risk; women are allowed and even required to be active in the defence of their chastity. Given that Villars is a clergyman it is particularly noteworthy that the threatened consequences for failing in this respect do not involve the wrath of God, but 'the censure of the world' and 'future regret' – the latter presumably arising from one's ruined chances in the marriage market.

Villars actually affirms the existence of the sexual double standard when he warns, 'Remember, my dear Evelina, *nothing* is so delicate as the reputation of a woman: it is at once, the most beautiful and most brittle of all human things'.[19] But speaking of female reputation in this manner – as if it were comparable to a piece of fine china – only serves to underline the thinking which informs the first perspective outlined at the beginning of this chapter. For Villars and all of the others propounding this outlook the only real value a single woman has depends entirely upon her maintaining 'unblemished chastity' and thus her reputation. Evelina may fight for her 'honour' but it is unthinkable that she should fight for her rights. Commenting upon Mme Duval's intention to force Evelina's father to fulfil his parental (that is, pecuniary) obligations via a lawsuit, Villars declares such a procedure to be 'totally repugnant to all female delicacy'. He has already indicated his position regarding the heroine and her future: 'My plan . . . was not merely to educate and to cherish her as my own, but to adopt her the heiress of my small fortune, and *to bestow her upon some worthy man*'.[20] Indeed, a 'worthy' man was – for any woman – considered the supreme reward for chastity and obedience by the supporters of model (1). Perhaps the biggest problem facing any woman lucky enough to attain this coveted prize was how to express sufficient gratitude to her magnanimous redeemer. Evelina, commenting on her wedding day ('the most important of my life!'), writes, 'Oh Lord Orville! – it shall be the sole study of my happy life, to express, better than by words, the sense I have of *your exalted benevolence*, and greatness of mind!'. Recounting the marriage she states, 'This morning, with fearful joy, and *trembling gratitude*, she united herself for ever with the object of her dearest, her eternal affection'.[21] From the terms used here one might – if not aware of the source – suppose this expression of thankfulness to be directed towards God, and not simply one's spouse.

I have suggested above that Evelina's genteel perspective requires that women ideally have a modicum of intelligence, but Burney is careful not to let the reader imagine that this trait is in itself a desirable attribute when found in women. It must not appear too salient, and therefore impair femininity; this is made manifest in

Evelina's description of Mrs Selwyn: 'She is extremely clever; her understanding, indeed, may be called *masculine*; but unfortunately, her manners deserve the same epithet; for, in studying to acquire the knowledge of the other sex, she has lost all the softness of her own'. Knowledge and a good understanding are here taken to be characteristically masculine whilst women are associated with the dubious trait of softness. The trouble with Mrs Selwyn – for the apologists of (1) – is that she lacks 'gentleness; a virtue which, nevertheless, seems so essential a part of the female character, that I find myself more awkward, and less at ease with a woman who wants it, than I do with a man'.[22] Evelina feels uneasy with such a woman because – presumably – she perceives the absence of gentleness in women as unnatural. Gentleness may not be expected of men (although a paragon like Lord Orville provides an exception) but it is a fundamental requirement for any real woman, being part of the trappings of submissiveness, deference and obedience – all demanded of women, particularly in their dealings with men. A good example of these qualities in *Evelina* is found in Mrs Mirvan, who, in spite of her husband's excesses, manages to epitomise unswerving femininity. As Orville approvingly remarks, 'She is gentle and amiable . . . a true feminine character'.[23]

Throughout the novel it is apparent that Evelina's fears and problems stem from her need to protect her reputation against various hazards whilst ensuring that Lord Orville receives and absorbs an appropriate impression of her worthiness. She must not simply *be* good but must also be *seen* to be good – this is a world wherein appearance, in every sense, is of the utmost importance; as Evelina is unfamiliar with the world, and more especially with the city, she has nothing to rely on but her own good heart and regular advice from her mentor, Villars. Notwithstanding the fact that he is a clergyman, Villars does not trouble himself – or the heroine – with very much religion; his letters to Evelina illustrate his grasp of bourgeois morality as opposed to any idealistic or other-worldly beliefs. In his view one's actions must be properly expedient in order to preserve one's image, and indeed Burney's characters make Erving Goffman's self-conscious actors appear positively nonchalant in their 'presentation of self'. As Villars points out in his anxious appraisal of Evelina's attempts to help McCartney, 'Where anything is doubtful, the ties of society, and the laws of humanity, claim a favourable interpretation; but remember, my dear child, that those of discretion have an equal claim to your regard'.[24] No mention here of religious duty, just contingent ties and laws which must always be balanced against discretion. This sums up the individualistic and instrumental nature of much eighteenth-century bourgeois moralising – all form and no moral content.

Religion then is notable in *Evelina* for its absence; all of the characters in the novel who display any concern about how their actions will be judged, are preoccupied with the opinions of their fellow-mortals and not with any religious code or deity. Secularisation is surely well advanced when one can create a character like Villars who, in spite of being a supposedly worthy minister, always bows to social pressure rather than religious ideals or convictions. For example, he does not want Evelina to go to London with Mme Duval, and is convinced that such a visit would be fraught with danger for the girl. However, rather than actively intervene to prevent the visit he merely mentions his reservations to Evelina and adds, 'But alas, my dear, we are the slaves of custom, the dupes of prejudice, and dare not stem the torrent of an opposing world, even though our own judgements condemn our compliance! however, since the die is cast, we must endeavour to make the best of it'.[25] Such an attitude is not that of one with any moral code, religious or otherwise: in fact it is closer to that stance which a contemporary sociologist has termed 'other-directed', and indicates the passivity and compliance of this fictitious churchman.[26] However, the fact that Burney could present a character of this type as an Anglican minister – and the character was readily accepted as plausible and worthy – is itself significant. For even if one were to argue that the Established Church of the period was not always accurately represented in fiction, there is no doubt that Villars was viewed as an authentic type of clergyman by Burney's audience.

The poor do not appear in *Evelina* unless one counts McCartney, who turns out to be Lord Belmont's son (and therefore Evelina's half-brother); apart from the petit-bourgeois Branghtons the only 'lower class' characters in the novel are servants. The most important reference to them occurs when Mme Duval is attacked during the 'robbery', and Evelina remarks to Villars, 'Her dress was in such disorder, that I was quite sorry to have her figure exposed to the servants, who all of them, in imitation of their master, hold her in derision'.[27] In spite of Mme Duval's 'vulgarity' then, Evelina still feels that it is unfortunate for her to be humiliated in front of the servants and goes on to make a clichéd comment about servants following the example of their employer. Mme Duval had – prior to her first marriage – been a member of the lower classes and this is held against her by both Villars and Lady Howard, who describe her as 'vulgar and illiterate', 'low-bred and illiberal', and do not for one moment forget that she was originally 'a waiting girl at a tavern'. Mr Evelyn, Mme Duval's first husband, had been urged by Villars et al. not to marry her and pays the price for succumbing to beauty over breeding as he dies two years after the marriage.[28]

Despite the fact that Evelina is said to be a rustic and is unfamiliar with society, she does have a strong sense of status. In her observations on Mme Duval and the Branghtons there is more than just moral disapproval – there is something which can only be described as snobbery or status-contempt. Writing to Villars, Evelina complains about the Branghtons, stating, 'I fear you will think this London journey has made me grow very proud, but indeed this family is so *low-bred and vulgar*, that I should be equally ashamed of such a connexion in the country, or anywhere'.[29] She is further upset that Sir Clement has seen her in the company of the Branghtons and Mme Duval, his opinion being valued because of his rank and his intimacy with Lord Orville: Sir Clement has, after all, made himself a thorough nuisance to Evelina prior to this, so her concern does not proceed from any respect or liking for *him*.[30] Sir Clement harrasses Evelina on yet another occasion, causing her anxiety over what Orville might suppose her relationship with Sir Clement to be – and yet, when Sir Clement sees her with the Branghtons for a second time, she goes on to state, 'nothing could be more disagreeable to me, than being seen by Sir Clement Willoughby with a party at once so vulgar in themselves, and so familiar to me'.[31] This attitude on Evelina's part rests upon her desire to favourably impress Orville and, more generally, her extreme consciousness of status; both factors characterise the heroine throughout the whole piece.

On moving into lodgings with Mme Duval, Evelina comments, 'I am sure that I have a thousand reasons to rejoice that I am so little known; for my present situation is, in every respect, very unenviable, and I would not, for the world, be seen by any acquaintance of Mrs Mirvan'.[32] One can be certain that Evelina's fear of being 'seen by any acquaintance of Mrs Mirvan' stems from a desire to maintain her own status position, and not from any apprehension that she might discredit Mrs Mirvan by association. On this, Evelina's second visit to London, the fact that she is in a different part of town with different companions leads her to view the place itself negatively, and to deem 'the inhabitants *illiterate and under-bred*'.[33] Indeed throughout the whole novel the unpolished Evelina – who claims to think of herself as a 'nobody' – describes others in this manner; her reputed humility never prevents her from using epithets such as 'inelegant and low-bred'.[34] After her initial encounter with Lovel, in which she makes a few social gaffes, Evelina writes, 'I think there ought to be a book, of the laws and customs *à-la-mode*, presented to all young people, upon their first introduction to public company', yet we can hardly see the heroine's need for this given that she has absorbed all of the major points relating to bourgeois manners from her guardian, and does not hesitate to judge those she meets according to whether or not they comply with this code.[35]

Evelina despises the Branghtons for trying to appear grander than they are, as much as for anything else; their attempts to impress her she assesses thus: 'Had they been without *pretensions*, all this would have seemed of no consequence; but they aimed at appearing to advantage, and even fancied they succeeded'.[36] Likewise when Smith tries to emulate the quality, Evelina writes, 'he was dressed in a very showy manner, but without any taste, and the inelegant smartness of his air and deportment, his visible struggle, against education, to put on the fine gentleman, added to his frequent conscious glancing at a dress to which he was but little accustomed, very effectually destroyed his aim of *figuring*, and rendered all his efforts useless'.[37] In other words, the petit-bourgeois should not ape their betters; the failure of such attempts to copy are as bad as – if not worse than – the intention to appear to be of a higher status than is strictly one's due. This rather clashes with Evelina's own endeavour to create a good impression upon Orville (she certainly tries to appear 'to advantage'), and does not match well with her own and Villars' ideas about 'prudence' and appearance. One cannot doubt that most of Evelina's delights and anxieties depend upon the impression which she thinks Lord Orville has of her. For example, although she does not seem to be embarrassed at inadvertently being in the company of whores when the Branghtons see her, she is mortified when Orville passes by and observes the same scene. Shortly afterwards, the coach incident and Tom Branghton's subsequent interview with Orville horrify the heroine still further: 'I was half frantic, I really raved; the good opinion of Lord Orville now seemed irretrievably lost'.[38]

In contrast to her contempt for the Branghtons and others, Evelina shows the greatest respect for the exemplary Orville, both for his social position and his personal qualities. Consequently she feels excited and anxious in the peer's presence; indeed on first learning that he is a nobleman she writes, 'This gave me new alarm; how will he be provoked, thought I, when he finds what a simple rustic he has *honoured with his choice!*' (all this because Orville has asked her to dance). Moreover, 'That he should be *so much my superior in every way*, quite disconcerted me'.[39] Evelina is clearly awed by the company of a social superior and therefore, 'I was quite ashamed of being so troublesome, and so much above myself as these seeming airs made me appear'.[40] Yet she need not have worried, for the sophistication which she attributes to the rich leads her to conclude that 'These people in high life have too much presence of mind, I believe, to *seem* disconcerted, or out of humour, however they may feel'. So, 'insignificant' as Evelina feels 'compared to a man of his rank and figure', she nevertheless decides to 'make the best of it'.[41]

Evelina soon discovers that not all persons of 'rank and figure' live up to her expectations concerning them; at the Pantheon she becomes uneasy when she realises that one of Orville's companions is openly leering at her: 'I was quite surprised, that a man whose boldness was so offensive, could have gained admission into a party of which Lord Orville made one; for *I naturally concluded him to be some low-bred, and uneducated man*'.[42] Naturally' because Evelina supposes that the quality monopolise not only money and power, but also manners, good conduct, and anything else she values. However, she then hears Sir Clement refer to the offender by his title, and her reaction is one of amazement, 'Lordship! – how extraordinary! that a *nobleman*, accustomed, in all probability, to the first rank of company in the kingdom, from his earliest infancy, can possibly be deficient in *good manners*, however faulty in morals and principles!'.[43] So, unlike servants, whose behaviour is dependent upon example, peers may fail to emulate the best qualities of the 'first rank of company' with which they are, surmises Evelina, familiar from birth. It is worth noting that Evelina can be startled by Merton's poor manners yet not expect that he – or any other noble – need be an adherent to sound 'moral and principles'. Once again appearance is shown to be more important in Evelina's world than actual conduct or moral stance. To understand the above incident she can only muse that we are all 'different', regardless of rank:

> In all ranks and all stations of life, how strangely do characters and manners differ! Lord Orville, with a politeness which knows no intermission, and makes no distinction, is as unassuming and

modest, as if he had never mixed with the great, and was totally
ignorant of every qualification he possesses; this other Lord, though
lavish of compliments and fine speeches, seems to me an entire
stranger to real good breeding.[44]

Thus humble Evelina, admirer of the nobility, feels no qualms about
assessing the breeding of her social superiors.

In one respect *Evelina* is a variation of the 'Cinderella' fairy-tale:
the (apparently) poor girl making good.[45] Whatever her true position, as Sir John Belmont's daughter, 'she has too little wealth to be
sought with propriety by men of the fashionable world', Villars tells
Lady Howard.[46] He further recognises that Evelina's circumstances
are not compatible with London and fashionable society, as, 'The
supposed obscurity of your birth and situation, makes you liable to
a thousand disagreeable adventures'. Not that Villars or Lady Howard
are complacent about Evelina's situation. When the former fails to
respond favourably to the proposal to approach Sir John on the
subject of Evelina, Lady Howard chides, 'Can it be right, my dear
Sir, that this promising young creature should be deprived of the
fortune, and rank of life, to which she is lawfully entitled, and which
you have prepared her to support and to use so nobly? To despise
riches, may, indeed, be philosophic, but to dispense them worthily,
must surely be more beneficial to mankind'.[47] The idea of riches as
something to be dispensed 'worthily' (or otherwise) does not, however, figure much in this novel; unlike Pamela, Evelina does not
waste any time pondering the performance of future good works.
And Lady Howard is obviously mistaken if she thinks that Villars
'despises' riches; he is extremely conscious of both social and economic distinctions and – for all of his hopes that Evelina will remain
unaffected by the city, and will end up living in the country – he
always has his eye on the main chance. Although he has earlier
spoken of the need to curb ambition as 'the first step to content-
ment', he immediately succumbs to Mme Duval's economic threats
concerning Evelina and reveals his true hopes for the girl when
justifying this compliance: 'The connections she may hereafter form,
the style of life for which she may be destined, and the future family
to which she may belong, are considerations which give but too
much weight to the menaces of Mme Duval'.[48] Clearly Villars is well
aware of the possibility of Evelina marrying into a higher class or
rank, in spite of his earlier pronouncements, and he shows no disapproval of such upward mobility. Were he really content for Evelina

to live simply with no other fortune than that which he could provide, then he would hardly take Mme Duval's threats seriously.
Additionally, he has no tangible reason to assume that Evelina will
be upwardly mobile when the above comment is made.

When Evelina is about to meet her father, Villars – who has
shifted from thinking that nothing would come of approaching Sir
John, to being convinced that the girl will be economically and
socially rewarded – again expresses the hope that she will remain
'unspoiled': 'may'st thou, in this change of situation, experience no
change of disposition! but receive with humility, and support with
meekness, the elevation to which thou art rising!'.[49] Money and high
status may be desirable but Villars believes that they need to be
handled carefully; consequently when Evelina is about to marry he
prays 'that the giddy height of bliss to which thou art rising may not
render thee giddy, but that the purity of thy mind may form the
brightest splendour of thy prosperity!'[50] Indeed to Burney's audience, especially the women, the view that a 'good' marriage (involving upward economic and social mobility plus security) was the
'height of bliss' was doubtless acceptable, for, as Evelina herself has
discovered, 'how requisite are birth and fortune to the attainment of
respect and civility'.[51]

9
Robert Bage:
Hermsprong (1796)

Literary critics have frequently portrayed Robert Bage as an ardent supporter of female emancipation. Kelly and Faulkner see him as such, and Wilkins states that Bage believed in 'the equality of woman with man' and 'championed the cause of sexual equality'.[1] Yet many of Bage's assumptions and attitudes regarding women were common currency among conservative thinkers of the period.

Caroline Campinet, the heroine in *Hermsprong*, largely conforms to the literary ideal of beauty, benevolence, propriety and obedience, although Bage suggests that her intelligence and interests make her atypical. Caroline only speaks at length on the subject of flattery, displaying both her disapproval and her susceptibility to it;[2] her overriding concern is with the demands of 'filial obedience'.[3] This leads her to choose duty towards her rascally father, Lord Grondale, before her love for Hermsprong – in spite of the 'reason' which the author attributes to her. Indeed her sense of duty is so strong that only Grondale's eventual death allows Caroline to act in accordance with both love and reason.[4]

Caroline's friend, Miss Fluart, is a far more interesting character who displays contempt for the 'female' traits of sulking and scolding, upsets Grondale's mistress, and encourages the heroine to abandon her passive obedience and commitment to 'transcendent duty'.[5] Miss Fluart also makes a fool of Grondale, openly scorns his suppositions concerning Hermsprong and Caroline, and defends the hero's attitude towards Caroline's aunt, Mrs Garnet. For Miss Fluart, who sees nothing wrong in cross-class marriages between rich women and poor men, the characteristic motivations of people of rank amount to little more than 'pride and avarice'.[6] However, Grondale sees Miss Fluart (and her £20,000) as an attractive proposition, and she loses no time in exploiting this fact.[7] The old tyrant does not appreciate how completely he has been used until Miss Fluart successfully masquerades as Caroline, allowing the heroine to escape an unwelcome arranged marriage.[8]

Miss Fluart then is quite different from Caroline; she is quick-witted, humorous, argumentative, sceptical and courageous; there is no hint of feebleness or hesitation in her character. This independent woman even demonstrates some understanding of the nature of female oppression when she ironically remarks: 'Our obligations to men are infinite. Under the name of father, or brother, or guardian, or husband, they are always protecting us from liberty'.[9] The 'wedding' is probably the most blatant example of Miss Fluart's spirit and determination. Not content with outraging Grondale, she then takes the opportunity to display her contempt for the sycophantic cleric, Blick, rubs salt into Grondale's wounds with further mockery, and then escapes, threatening to shoot anyone who hinders her.[10] She remains unmarried at the conclusion of the novel – in the absence of another Hermsprong she is, as Bage puts it, 'not yet willing "to buy herself a master"'.[11]

Wilkins clearly shows his preference for Miss Fluart when he writes, 'I wish Bage had made her his heroine. I do indeed'.[12] Given that she is more in keeping with the ideal outlined by Hermsprong one may wonder why Bage did not. There are several possibilities. In spite of Bage's 'egalitarian' stance he may have employed a conventional heroine simply because his real conception of a desirable woman was less radical than his rhetoric. On the other hand he may have felt that an emancipated female character, whilst being of interest to readers, would find little favour as a heroine. It is possible – although extremely unlikely given the nature of *Hermsprong* – that Bage sought verisimilitude in portraying the submissive manner often demanded of daughters during the period. I reiterate the discrepancy between Hermsprong's ideal/Bage's 'feminism' and the heroine in order to suggest that Caroline is interchangeable with virtually any other middle-class or aristocratic/gentry heroine found in eighteenth-century English novels. She could certainly change places with the heroines in *Amelia*, *David Simple* or *The Vicar of Wakefield*, to name but three. Bage's supposed feminism finds no expression in his heroine, who is so completely conventional and conservative a creation that she even faints when her life is in danger.[13]

Hermsprong's contact with the Sumelin family provides some interesting instances of how Bage represents women. Mrs Sumelin is vain and stupid, her eldest daughter, Harriet, being 'a perfect copy of her mother; fond to excess of the fine and fashionable, and an adorer of sweet pretty things'. Bage sees such propensities among women as 'part of the constitution of their natures'.[14] However, as Sumelin's youngest daughter, Charlotte, is a close friend of Miss Fluart and can therefore be assumed not to share such traits, Bage appears to be describing 'innate' female characteristics that do not even remain constant among women of the same family!

Mr Sumelin is portrayed as something of a misogynist who, on hearing that Harriet has eloped with a 'coxcomb', comments: 'we must set that down as a circumstance in Harriet's favour, coxcombry being the most approved qualification of man, in the mind of woman'.[15] Hermsprong eventually persuades Harriet to abandon her lover and return home, and in so doing he employs a good deal of deceit; Bage suggests that this is justifiable when dealing with women 'on certain great occasions'.[16] Harriet's pique at returning is exacerbated when her attempts to captivate Hersmprong fail: this 'made her his enemy for life'.[17] Bage's presentation of this episode strongly suggests that he considers Harriet's pride and selfishness to be fairly representative of young women in general.

In a later conversation between the Sumelins, Hermsprong, Caroline and Miss Fluart, the latter asks Hermsprong if he thinks the subject of politics improper for women, to which he replies: 'I think no subject improper for ladies, which ladies are qualified to discuss, *if their fathers first, and then themselves, so pleased*'. Hermsprong is obviously voicing a patriarchal attitude here. It leads Mr Sumelin to claim that 'Women have too much liberty', and Hermsprong agrees that 'English young ladies of a certain age and rank have too much liberty of person'. But, he adds, 'they have too little liberty of mind'. By this he means that their minds are preoccupied with fashionable events and places such as Ranelagh, and it is apparent that his concern is with bourgeois and aristocratic/gentry women; neither Bage nor his hero waste any time considering the 'liberty' available to working women.[18]

In Hermsprong's view it is necessary for women to be better educated, and for men to *demand more of women intellectually*; additionally, he argues that children should be raised in a way which involves 'less distinction of sex'. At this point Sumelin, generalising from his own experience, states: 'There are two things co-existent with women, and co-eternal; admiration of fineries and of themselves'. The hero's rejoinder is instructive: 'women would leave the lesser vanities, and learn lessons of wisdom, *if men would teach them;*

and in particular, this, that more permanent and more cordial happiness might be produced to both the sexes, *if the aims of women were rather to obtain the esteem of men, than that passionate yet transient affection usually called love'*.[19] It is clear that whilst Hermsprong opposes Sumelin's negative outlook, he can only envisage the education of women as a process in which men are forever the teachers and women the pupils. Indeed Hermsprong's argument can be interpreted as meaning no more than that women could (and should) become more worthy companions for men, an idea favoured in the early part of the century by Defoe. The rationale behind this sort of perspective depends upon increasing the usefulness and potential of women *for the benefit of men*; it does not see intellectual progress as an end in itself or an intrinsically valuable goal for women.

Whilst Hermsprong does suggest that certain 'masculine' virtues (such as intelligence) can be proper goals for women, we soon learn that 'compassion for the unfortunate, accompanied with benevolence, was precisely what, in Mr. Hermsprong's opinion, raised the female character to the highest degree of perfection'.[20] These are very conventional 'female' virtues and Hermsprong's sentiments were undoubtedly shared with those who felt no sympathy whatsoever for any form of egalitarianism.

Recounting his past life in America, Hermsprong speaks of the 'aborigines' with evident approval, particularly the women: 'the *modesty* of their young women is uncommon. They have *delicacy* also; and respecting men, a *timidity* of which here I have not seen many examples'. Modesty, delicacy and timidity are here taken to be virtues. However, the praise of such attributes surely has little place in the construction of an egalitarian or 'feminist' case for women. Miss Fluart challenges Hermsprong for advocating timidity, but he replies that his main recommendation for women is that they acquire 'minds to reason, understandings to judge', thus, 'propriety of action must follow of necessity'.[21] In this way they can become 'heavenly women' like Miss Fluart and Caroline – his 'lovely hearers'.

The hero goes on to consider the notion of reciprocity/contract in order to argue that Grondale has negated any obligations on Caroline's part, but this leads Miss Fluart to quiz Hermsprong on the sexual double standard. If I were your wife and you were unfaithful to me, she asks, would I then have the right to be unfaithful to you? He replies, 'Yes, my most charming creature in the universe, yes, as far as respects myself. But, in this case, *you have contracted an obliga-*

tion with society also. Society does not think itself so much injured by the lapse of the male. In short, you bear the children. To you I need not point out the important deductions from this single circumstance'.[22] Yet whilst the biological fact of women bearing children is here presented as the basis for female obligation to the reification 'society', it is not clear why a *social* duty should follow from such a fact. If Hermsprong means that custom and tradition must be obeyed, then this opinion is at variance with the scorn which he typically displays towards unjust or ridiculous conventions and practices. As Stone has observed, by the end of the eighteenth century, contraceptive techniques were definitely available (for example, the condom had been introduced one hundred years previously), even if they were not widely practised.[23] Additionally, wealthy women would have been able to get any illegitimate progeny 'adopted'; this was frequently done in cases of male adultery. Alternatively there is the argument put to Boswell, who, objecting to female sexual equality on the issue of adultery, argued for the importance of property rights and the need to ensure the legitimacy of heirs. His protagonist replied, 'that is easily answered, for the objection is removed if a woman does not intrigue but when she is with child'. As Boswell later admitted, 'I really could not answer her'.[24] The fact is that Hermsprong argues *for* the double standard and in the course of his polemic shifts his focus from the idea of a contract between husband and wife to that of one between wives and society.

The above examples of the author's attitude towards women could be multiplied ad nauseum and, in my view, make Bage an unlikely champion of women; even the minor female characters in *Hermsprong* do not escape his contempt. There is Miss Brown, who foolishly elopes; Miss Bentley, with her ironic attitude towards love; Mrs Merrick who, once jilted, becomes deeply distrustful of all men for the rest of her life.[25] In addition there is the 'weak' Mrs Garnet (whom Hermsprong chides for, amongst other things, her lack of 'manly spirit'); Hermsprong's own mother, with her religious bigotry; Sir Philip Chestrum's mother, who is in turn domineering and obsequious, and finally, Mrs Stone, Grondale's vain and cunning concubine.[26] Moreover, whilst one of the characters critical of women, Mr Woodcock, is satirised by Bage, the former's wife is also presented as an unpleasant and stupid person. Bage outlines the ideal female as envisaged by Woodcock with a view to deriding him, particularly by comparing this ideal to Woodcock's actual wife. Nevertheless, what is here shown as a ludicrously idealistic construction of woman differs very little from Bage's portrayal of Caroline Campinet. If Woodcock's ideal is absurd then so is the author's heroine. We are told that Mrs Woodcock is cruel, but Bage seems to be interested in sneering at her largely because she 'had been a virgin for ten years longer than the fitness of things required', that is, she had been an 'old maid'.[27] Bage's supposed sympathy for women did not prevent him from utilising this unfavourable stereotype of women unable or unwilling to marry. Even though we are invited to laugh at the near-misogyny of both Woodcock and Sumelin, they are characterised as good men albeit with discreditable wives.

Bage's radicalism cannot even be shown to be particularly critical of religion; as noted above, Woodcock, (an Anglican minister) may be a figure of fun but he is by no means a bad man; Hermsprong has a high opinion of him and is quite prepared to support him.[28] Similarly, Parson Brown – who adopts the narrator, Gregory Glen – is a compassionate and generous man, as is shown by his attempt to protect the young Glen's interests, and by his will.[29] The religious villain in the novel is Dr Blick, a careerist who is also a JP and a lackey for Lord Grondale. Glen describes Blick as follows: 'he united pride with meanness; . . . he was as haughty to his inferiors as cringing to superiors; an eternal flatterer of Lord Grondale, he did not even presume to preach against a vice, if it happened to be a vice of his patron'. Nevertheless, when Hermsprong asks Glen if Blick is typical of the Anglican clergy Glen replies: 'as individuals, I think them generally worthy'.[30] Hermsprong subsequently raises this question again and Glen suggests that – apart from a little religious bigotry – clergymen are 'in general rather amiable than otherwise'. Returning to Blick however, Glen speaks of the minister's 'love of accumulation', and adds, 'the doctor knows that it is his duty rather to govern than to teach his flock'.[31]

One might argue that this was the function of all eighteenth-century Anglican clergymen, but neither Glen nor Hermsprong make this sort of general or structural criticism of the Established Church. Consequently Bage leaves his readers with the idea that what is at issue is the personality or character of individual religious functionaries, and in so doing he avoids, ignores, or fails to understand the institutionalised role of the Church in eighteenth-century England. In this account, the only thing wrong with the Church is the fact that it contains some corrupt and selfish individuals; the author therefore fails to locate the Church within a system of domination which operated to maintain inequality between classes in favour of a small élite of aristocrats, the gentry, and the upper bourgeoisie. Complicity with, and subservience to, local nobles was not simply the practice of a few corrupt ministers; Blick's conniving with Grondale, his abuse of his position as a JP, and his exploitation of Woodcock, represent a general pattern which can only be understood when placed within the context of class domination during the period, and not viewed – as Bage's perspective implies – as the vices of one atypical clergyman.[32] In the character of Blick, Bage has merely given the reader a clerical scoundrel and not – as one might expect from a radical – a critique of the Church, however modest.

Blick continually bemoans the lack of reverence shown towards the clergy and labels anyone who does not fully agree with his opinions as an atheist or political subversive. Woodcock's lack of support for him during an encounter with Glen and Hermsprong leads to Blick sacking Woodcock and claiming that he is 'tainted with principles almost republican'. This incident occurs after a heated argument between Blick and Hermsprong in which the former contends that human nature dictates that 'Man must fear death'. Our hero, who has already pointed out that the American 'savages' do *not* fear death, wishes to maintain that the most important conditioning factor relating to this issue is what we might now term socialisation. This is not to ignore natural determinations, for, 'Man cannot be taught anything contrary to nature. However he acts, he must act by nature's laws'.[33] In this way Hermsprong displays his relativistic position, claiming that anything which human beings do *must* be natural; this is in sharp contrast to Blick's conception of a clearly discernible, fixed human nature, operating independently from historical and cultural variables. So, on this point, Bage places his hero firmly within a tradition of enlightened or 'progressive' thought, whilst Blick struggles to defend conservative determinism.

Hermsprong further wishes to assert that: 'to a reflecting mind, at least death is not an evil', and this lures Blick into a tangle of contradictions, for he wants to count death as an evil whilst also proposing that 'it is enlargement of sensation. It is renovation – it is the gate of life – it is a passport to eternal joys'. As Hermsprong points out, if Blick's above statement is true, then death cannot possibly be an evil. The minister is unpleasantly surprised to find himself thus defeated, and so concludes that the hero has been influenced by 'the abominable doctrines of the French philosophers'.[34]

Blick's mean-spirited character is amplified when a storm ravages the village of Grondale; as Hermsprong tries to give the victims some practical assistance, all that Blick can do is utter pious words and denigrate the hero's efforts because they do not proceed from 'faith'. In conversation with Lord Grondale the minister bemoans the passing of former ages, in which he supposes that servility to those of his class and profession was more extensive and firmly established, and goes on to help the former to 'prove' the laudable character of consuetudinage.[35] With his thinly-veiled support for the anniversary of reactionary riots against Dissenters – which actually took place in Birmingham in 1791 – and his long tirade against those whom he assumes to be influenced by 'atheistical lawgivers of a neighbouring country', Blick makes his position perfectly clear.[36] 'Failure of respect' for the ruling class and its institutions (especially the Church) threatens to lead to 'the overthrow of all religion, all government, all that is just and equitable on earth'.[37]

These utterances only show what Blick is; they hardly constitute an appraisal of the eighteenth-century Established Church and its ministers. In a novel such as *Hermsprong* this must be counted as a failing and, in spite of the criticism of some of Bage's more reactionary reviewers, it is obvious that Bage is not really against religion (including Anglicanism) at all. Indeed he attributes a number of positive functions to it, suggesting via his hero that it teaches 'love and goodwill', and that the (alleged) acceptance of widely differing opinions in America arises from 'their diversity of religions, which, accustoming them to see differences of opinion in a matter of the greatest importance, disposes them to tolerate it on all subjects, and even to believe it a condition of human nature'. In this section Hermsprong seems to be claiming that it is the unchristian nature of English politics which makes the English people intolerant; in fact, throughout the novel the only negative comments about religion refer to nunneries and to the converting zeal of Hermsprong's mother.[38]

But what of rank? Surely Bage – as an egalitarian – is radical on this issue? There is no doubt that he wants to poke fun at the aristocracy, as his account of Sir Philip Chestrum and Sir John shows; the latter is a dull-witted rake, whilst Sir Philip is ugly, mean, snobbish and a gambler – he even has the stigma of his father having been 'in trade'. However, most of the criticism Bage aims at the aristocracy is directed at Lord Grondale, whose pastimes include drinking, gambling and, if I interpret Bage's reference to mercury correctly, lechery.[39]

When Grondale first meets Hermsprong, shortly after the hero has saved Caroline's life, his first concern is Hermsprong's rank; in

answer to the peer's enquiry the hero states: 'As to rank, – I have
been taught only to distinguish men by virtue'.[40] Such remarks coupled with a noticeable lack of deference ensure Grondale's animos-
ity. Lord Grondale's preoccupation with rank coincides with his
distaste for the developing bourgeois economy: 'A fine thing this
commerce . . . it doubles production, and enlarges all sorts of qualities but good ones'. He even attributes Miss Fluart's sauciness to the
same cause: 'The girl is a child of commerce, and thinks, to be young,
to be a hoyden, and to have a fortune, excuses everything'.[41] However Bage is obviously promoting certain bourgeois interests, and it
is perhaps for this reason that Squire Grooby, Sir Philip, Sir John and
Lord Grondale are presented in such a distinctly unfavourable light
vis-à-vis bourgeois virtues, many of which are epitomised by
Hermsprong.[42] The latter reiterates and augments his initial comments on the importance of virtue, as opposed to rank, throughout
the novel, with pronouncements such as this: 'I cannot learn to offer
incense at the shrines of wealth and power, nor at any shrines but
those of probity and virtue'. Moreover, Hermsprong has read Paine's
Rights of Man, something which Grondale's lawyer, Corrow, hopes
to cite as evidence that the hero is a foreign spy.[43]

In addition to his criticisms regarding rank, Hermsprong also
casts some doubt upon the desirability of the type of society emerging in England, arguing that whilst English cities may be 'magnifi-
cent' they are also full of poverty. Furthermore, the benefits arising
from 'progress' which are so admired by Glen and Woodcock (mainly
those in art and science) are not, states the hero, available to the
'common people'; such people can be happy if 'unoppressed by
labour or poverty' and they – like the 'native Americans' – are at
least free from the boredom and incapacity for happiness Hermsprong
associates with rich Europeans. He goes on to assert that certain
'European' skills such as reading would not be of much use to the
'aborigines', as so much reading-matter is neither pleasurable nor
enlightening.[44] Both they and the common people of England with
whom they are compared are here considered unlikely to gain anything from the acquisition of literacy; education is not an unequivocal good for Hermsprong. It is one thing to be in favour of a broad
artistic and scientific education for the daughters of the aristocracy,
gentry, and bourgeoisie, but quite another thing to advocate education for all.

Hermsprong's criticisms of English society suggest little in the
way of social change; he is concerned with individual rather than
social phenomena, stating: 'I must be independent, as far as social

man can be independent'.[45] For a happier society, 'Manners must change much, and governments more', but regarding the latter he goes on to bluntly claim that 'governments do not change, at least for the better'. Any significant change is seen as arising from within individuals and not changes in the social structure, and throughout the novel social issues are interpreted in psychological/individual terms. Poor government is seen as proceeding from widespread addiction to 'pleasure and luxury', which can lead to 'political care-lessness' and thus to 'political corruption'; Hermsprong's undeveloped solution is 'Simple government'.[46]

The conflict between Hermsprong and Lord Grondale reaches a climax in the court scene in which the peer, with the help of Blick and Corrow, hopes to prove that the hero is a subversive who has incited the miners to riot.[47] The charge cannot be substantiated; a junior justice present at the riot recounts Hermsprong's words to the miners, and we can see the nature of the hero's radicalism by synopsising his speech to them: (1) Your wages may be inadequate for 'superfluities' but times are hard; (2) Not everyone can be rich and *equality of property is impossible*; (3) Any attempt to achieve such equality would involve 'scenes of guilt and horror' which would ultimately destroy you too; (4) The rich have luxury, but also diseases – your poverty is offset by good health; why wish for the former?[48]

The above is the argument of a reactionary rather than that of an egalitarian; the unsupported claims that it includes are that the miners seek equality and superfluities, and not simply to maintain their standard of living above that of extreme poverty. Yet Bage has previously told the reader that the unrest stems from the high cost of provisions.[49] Hermsprong does nothing to demonstrate or justify his assertion that equality of property is an impossibility. Neither does he show that the expropriation of the wealthy necessarily leads to the destruction of those who dare to do it. Finally, there is no reason why wealth and power should automatically lead to disease; on the other hand, poverty has never been known for its health-giving properties outside the realm of ruling-class and bourgeois rhetoric. This claim about the correlation between health and poverty was frequently made by eighteenth-century novelists (Richardson, Gold-smith et al.), but the regularity with which it appears does nothing to make it any more plausible.

It is obvious that Hermsprong has argued for the status quo, but this was not enough to save Bage from the harsh judgement of a nineteenth-century commentator who wrote: 'he systematically made his novels the vehicle of all the anti-social, anti-moral, and anti-religious theories that were then but too much in vogue amongst the half-educated classes in this country'.[50] More recent critics display a variety of opinions; Allen describes Bage as having 'thorough-going radical and French revolutionary sympathies', whilst Wilkins, in his preface to the Turnstile edition of *Hermsprong*, expresses the view that Bage was 'a radical and not a revolutionary'. Wilkins admits to being puzzled as to why Sir Walter Scott – who apparently thought that *Hermsprong* was Bage's best work – did not select the novel for Ballantyne's 'Novelists Library'. As *Hermsprong* is generally taken to be Bage's most radical novel, and Scott was never known for his progressive opinions, it is curious that Wilkins does not draw the obvious conclusion. Some twentieth-century critics assure us that Bage was a decent fellow after all; Faulkner, for example, suggests that Hermsprong's stance against the miners illustrates 'Moderation of political outlook', and goes on to write of the hero's 'Burkean sentiments'. Burke and moderation is a combination which would not have occurred to this writer, but no matter; at least Faulkner recognises that 'Bage's attitude is more bourgeois than revolution-ary: he is anxious to avoid disturbances and strengthen "civil order"'.[51]

Kelly rightly perceives that Bage was articulating largely middle-class values, and also seeks to explain why Bage did not, generally speaking, suffer the harsh assessment which contemporary critics made of other radical writers. Firstly, Kelly suggests that Bage's 'social and political criticism' was – in view of its humour – 'advan-tageously ambiguous'; moreover, according to Kelly, Bage escaped censure because he was geographically distant from 'the centre of political passions in London'.[52] One explanation which Kelly does not accept is that Bage was not very radical, and he warns the reader that 'it is entirely wrong to see him as a secret conservative'. Regard-ing the humour of Bage's work I think that Kelly is missing a funda-mental point, for he further claims that if one considered the novels in their social context *and left out the humour*, then one would appre-ciate just how radical Bage really was.[53] The short answer to this sort of statement is that Bage himself did not leave out the humour; moreover, his humour may well have had a somewhat different effect to that attributed to it by Kelly. That is to say, rather than seeing Bage as a radical, whose sense of humour ensured that even his political opponents were charmed by his work, it may be more

accurate to surmise that – partly because of his humour in conjunction with his articulation of bourgeois values, and partly because of
the comparatively conservative content of his pronouncements –
Bage was not considered to be in earnest. His humour did not so
much 'soften' his political views as empty his work of any threatening political content.[54]

One cannot consider *Hermsprong* apart from the humour in the
text because the humour and the writer's decision to employ it have
political implications. Perhaps Kelly is right to warn us against
labelling Bage a 'secret conservative'; it is more fruitful to see him as
a bourgeois radical who adhered to a number of openly conservative
tenets – a fact which has been ignored by, or has eluded, twentieth-
century critics (Allen, Wilkins, Kelly), or has been counted as 'moderation' (Faulkner), or 'civilised tolerance' (Sutherland), and ap-
plauded. Tripathi does not fall into this trap; he writes: 'the hero's
sympathies for the French Revolution are equivocal, and he is as
much for law and order, as much for King and Constitution as a
thoroughbred Tory might be'. And, 'The freedom that Bage and his
class were asking for meant no more than the extension of their
privilege *vis-à-vis* the Government and the ruling oligarchy'. As
Tripathi correctly claims, 'Hermsprong's defence in the trial scene is
a recantation, a loud disclaimer of genuine or alleged jacobinical
principles and sympathies'.[55]

When we left Hermsprong he was pacifying the miners; he goes
on to show that he not only opposes their collective protest ('riot-
ing'), but is also an avid supporter of the monarchy. One of the
crowd accuses him of being a spy for the King, 'and no better than
your master'. Hermsprong, the egalitarian, physically attacks this
individual and then tells him: 'so to revile your *King* is to weaken the
concord that ought to subsist betwixt him and all his *subjects*, and
overthrow all *civil* order'.[56] If there were no other evidence to indicate the limited extent of Hermsprong's radicalism, and his support
for deeply conservative opinions and institutions, this would, I maintain, be sufficient to illustrate the hero's acceptance of the established order. To cap this, Bage – for all his sneers at the aristocracy –
then reveals that Hermsprong is of noble birth, and the true owner
of Grondale's estate.[57]

In spite of these factors Allen has argued that the novel is 'a
completely intransigent attack on feudalism and the notion of aristocracy'.[58] I count such intransigence as something less than complete, and consider Bage to be just one step removed from those
members of the eighteenth-century bourgeoisie who – whilst wish-

ing to condemn the supposed depravity of male aristocrats – remained firm monarchists, envious of the privileges and power of the aristocracy. Bourgeois criticism of the aristocracy had more than a touch of jealousy about it, but it was nearly always the moral standards of the élite which were held up for disapproval, not the high status and power of people of rank. The problem, as seen by bourgeois commentators, was simply that *the wrong people had power, wealth and respect*; there was little opposition to the existence of inequality in all major spheres. Genuinely radical and vigorous critiques of the monopoly of wealth and power have typically been the prerogative of radicals far outside the mainstream of bourgeois thinking – those whom the bourgeoisie themselves would label 'revolutionaries'. And, as a number of twentieth-century literary critics have been anxious to point out, Bage was no revolutionary.

In order to be absolutely fair to Bage, and to properly understand his position within eighteenth-century English radicalism, it is instructive to compare the views expressed in *Hermsprong* with those of William Godwin and Thomas Paine – two of the foremost radicals of the period. Firstly, on the issue of 'simple government' (which Hermsprong advocates without giving any details) we can agree with Veitch when he writes: 'Burke said that the simple governments were radically defective. Godwin, on the contrary, held that, in government, every departure from simplicity was an evil to be deplored'.[59] Paine, writing not merely of government but of 'simple democracy', argued that it was impractical in the modern world and that the solution was 'ingrafting representation upon democracy'.[60] Whilst Godwin admitted that violence could lead to important sociostructural changes, he further claimed that 'revolutions, instead of being truly beneficial to mankind, answer no other purpose, than that of marring the salutary and uninterrupted progress, which might be expected to attend upon political truth and social improvement'. This distaste for violence and a belief in the power of 'reason' led Godwin to assume that there would be gradual but inevitable progress in his society. He concluded: 'The only method according to which social improvements can be carried on, with sufficient prospect of an auspicious event, is, when the improvement of our institutions advances, *in a just proportion to the illumination of the public understanding*'.[61] Hermsprong, although he does not accept the idea of progress quite so readily, likewise eschews violence and bases his hope for reform upon reason.

Paine implicitly recognised that force might be required to effect the 'general revolution in the principle of government' which he advocated. He felt that force was at least partly vindicated in view of the fact that: 'Sovereignty, as a matter of right, appertains to the nation only, and not to any individual; and *a nation has at all times an inherent and indefeasible right to abolish any form of government it finds inconvenient, and establish such as accords with its interest, disposition, and happiness*'.[62] The issue of sovereignty brings us back to Hermsprong: he supports the monarchy and argues that civil order is dependent upon concord between the king and his subjects. Neither Godwin nor Paine thought monarchy desirable. The former considered it to be 'founded in imposture', and stated that 'The true interest of man, requires the annihilation of factitious and imaginary distinctions; it is inseparable from monarchy to support and render them more palpable than ever'.[63] Paine, who was unswervingly hostile to the institution, wrote of 'Monarchical sovereignty, the enemy of mankind', and added, 'That monarchy is all a bubble, a mere court artifice to procure money, is evident (at least to me) in every character in which it can be viewed'. He maintained that 'We must shut our eyes against reason, we must basely degrade our understanding, not to see the folly of what is called monarchy'.[64]

Hermsprong – himself an aristocrat – does not oppose the institution of aristocracy. Yet Godwin remarked that 'The features of an aristocratical institution are two; privilege, and an aggravated monopoly of wealth. The first of these is the essence of aristocracy; the second, that without which aristocracy can rarely be supported. *They are both of them in direct opposition to all sound morality, and all generous independence of character*'.[65] Paine argued that whilst a title was, in itself, 'perfectly harmless', 'All hereditary *government* is in its nature tyranny'; he likewise contrasted 'government by election and representation' to that of 'monarchy and aristocracy', and observed that they represented the direct opposition of 'Reason and Ignorance'.[66]

To return to the 'independence' mentioned by Godwin, above, it is worth noting that he also suggested that '*individuality* is of the very essence of intellectual excellence', and claimed that, 'He is the most perfect man to whom *society is not a necessary of life*, but a luxury, innocent and enviable, in which he joyfully indulges'.[67] Hermsprong has a similarly individualistic view of the matter (in spite of supporting aristocracy), but Paine clearly opposed such a position when he argued that 'The mutual dependence and reciprocal interest which man has upon man, and all parts of a civilised community upon each other, create that great chain of connection which holds it together'. Moreover, 'Man is so naturally a creature of society, that it is almost

impossible to put him out of it'.[68] In short, Paine did not accept the
naive and ill-considered type of individualism which considered
society (in the sense of 'company' *or* meaning the totality of social
relations) as a burden upon the individual. Hermsprong, as illustrated above, is for religion but not in favour of religious conformity;
both Godwin and Paine shared this approach.[69] Godwin even discussed the issue of how far death could be seen as an 'evil', possible
providing the inspiration for the discussion of that topic in
Hermsprong.[70] Of the three, only Paine believed that workers should
be allowed to pursue the best deal which they could get for the sale
of their labour; he opposed statutory wage-control, and remarked,
'Why not leave them as free to make their own bargains, as the law-
makers are to let their farms and houses? Personal labour is all the
property they have'.[71]

Godwin, though stating nothing specific on the issue of female
emancipation in his *Enquiry Concerning Political Justice*, argued against
'The evil of marriage, as it is practiced in European countries', and
suggested that, 'The abolition of the present system of marriage,
appears to involve no evils' (an argument not strengthened by his
subsequent marriage to Mary Wollstonecraft).[72] We have already
considered the limitations of Hermsprong's position on female emancipation. When we turn to 'An Occasional Letter on the Female Sex'
(an anonymous piece probably not written by Paine himself, but
published in a magazine which he edited), which is indicative – as
Foner maintains – of Paine's interest in the subject, we find a considerably more radical approach.[73] The author states that 'If we take a
survey of ages and of countries, we shall find the women, almost –
without exception – at all times and in all places, adored and oppressed'.[74] The writer goes on to consider the plight of American-
Indian women and points out that they 'are what the Helots were
amongst the Spartans, a vanquished people, obliged to toil for their
conquerors. Hence on the banks of the Oroonoko, we have seen
mothers slaying their daughters out of compassion, and smothering
them in their hour of birth. They consider this barbarous pity as a
virtue'.[75] This contrasts markedly with the idyllic picture of Ameri-
can-Indian life drawn by Hermsprong – though it may explain the
'timidity regarding men' which he attributed to such women. The
author concludes:

Even in countries where they may be esteemed most happy, con-
strained in their desires in the disposal of their goods, robbed of

freedom of will by the laws, the slaves of opinion, which rules them with absolute sway, and construes the slightest appearances into guilt; surrounded on all sides by judges, who are at once tyrants and their seducers, and who, after having prepared their faults, punish every lapse with dishonour – nay, usurp the right of degrading them on suspicion! Who does not feel for the tender sex?[76]

This is a far more forceful attack upon the oppression of women than appears in *Hermsprong*.

From the foregoing comparison it is clear that Paine was the most radical of these three 'egalitarians'; the fictional Hermsprong is closer to Godwin's position than to that of Paine, but nevertheless, even Godwin's views on the aristocracy and the monarchy appear advanced compared to those of Bage's hero. In judging *Hermsprong* and thus – to some extent – Bage, one must consider the fact that some English and Scottish radicals had been subjected to severe persecution immediately prior to the publication of the novel (although Godwin had published his 'Enquiry' without too much trouble). The 'Two Acts' of 1794 facilitated legal prosecution, for, 'The first made spoken and written words, although not followed by any overt act, a treasonable practice; the second forbade all public meetings of which notice had not been given by resident householders'.[77] Moreover, as Veitch goes on to point out, 'The cause of reform was discredited in England because reformers were thought to approve of violence in France', and one may well sympathise with Bage for not wishing to be seen to advocate the sort of violence which – by 1796 – horrified many of those in England who had initially welcomed the French Revolution.[78] Nevertheless, I think that one must ultimately conclude that Bage was not – in comparison to his radical contemporaries – very radical himself, and was nowhere near as progressive as some subsequent commentators would have us believe.[79]

10

The Exalted Heroine and the Triumph of Order

In each of the novels discussed in this study there is evidence of the authors' tendency to promote an idealised model of the 'good' woman. The qualities attributed to these heroines may include philanthropy, loyalty, obedience and so on, but more generally they are shown as constituting a powerful moral force simply by their presence. All the heroines have high moral status, and in some cases (such as those of Pamela and Amelia) are morally superior to their men. In three of the works (*Pamela*, *Amelia*, *The Spiritual Quixote*) the moral strength of the heroine plays a major part in 'converting' and subsequently supporting the major male character. In all the novels, the heroine's worthiness ensures that she is viewed 'meritocratically', is eventually rewarded with a suitable partner, and – where appropriate – is allowed to achieve upward social mobility. Heroines are materially rewarded in all the novels except *The Spiritual Quixote* and *Hermsprong* (and in the former, minor heroines receive such rewards).

The authors did not apply the same criteria when assessing worthy, low-status male characters: their moral goodness was apparently not thought to be a sufficient reason for an improved social position. However, on the basis of individual excellence women could justifiably be incorporated into a higher class than that of their origin. It must be stressed here that the conception of social mobility found in these works was one of uplifting the outstanding individual as a favour or reward, and did not imply any concession to the working or middle classes *as a right*. Women could thus be – in a limited manner – the focal point of a certain amount of class compromise: compromise which was possible (and much blunted) in view of the fact that it occurred as a purely individual reward bestowed upon a particular woman, by a member of the ruling class. In this way the authors could write about upward social mobility without actually challenging the status quo; they offered, perhaps, some gratification for the individual's hopes and ambitions, whilst denying the idea that they sought to change the social order. These writers may have considered moral worth to be an end in itself, but the praise and adoration enjoyed by their heroines is usually accompanied by socio-economic advancement.

I have argued above that the most fundamental feature of the heroine in the novels examined was her laudable moral character; this is more important than anything she does, including giving alms to the poor. Heroines were not expected to be very active in the wider world, and were certainly not considered fit to engage in economic or political activities, or anything else which might be thought to compromise 'female delicacy'. Therefore, outside of the moral and domestic spheres, the heroines are condemned to a largely passive existence. Even Pamela – who is perhaps the most active of the heroines – is confined to struggling over her 'virtue', and here she reacts to, rather than initiates, the action. The heroine's removal from any meaningful activity in the outside world was the price she paid for the changing (and more favourable) assessment of her moral worth, and her socio-economic success. This was a form of exaltation which denied the exalted any genuine power, and the reward itself was dependent upon the heroine's acceptance of a continuing reliance upon – and obedience to – her male benefactor. For example, the very independence which Pamela displays when opposing B. must be much modified prior to her absorption into the gentry. She cannot maintain the same degree of independence and moral autonomy – the qualities which supposedly distinguished her from other women, and made her attractive to B. – but must eschew them in order to claim her reward. Viewed in this light, the exaltation of the heroine looks less like the victory of female excellence within a romantic context, less like the breaking-down of class barriers through the power of love, and more like the possession and control of desirable women (regardless of class) by means of socio-economic bribery, the containment (or harmless channelling) of middle-class aspirations, and the maintenance of existing social, political and economic relations.

Both Watt and Spacks have commented upon the novelty of Richardson's portrayal of a servant-girl who holds chastity to be a prime value. I have suggested that he synthesised this and associated values and qualities in order to construct a fairly innovative paradigm for women generally. The claim that the ideal outlined by Richardson (and subsequently adopted by most eighteenth-century prose-fiction writers) was new – particularly in its application – can be supported with reference to the treatment of women in earlier English literature. Haskell has described the contrasting images of women of different social positions in the literature of the late Medieval period thus: 'if a woman were poor she was expected to be more vulnerable to temptation than a woman of higher birth; if she were a queen she was expected to be a shadowy sketch of the Virgin'.[1] Richetti, writing of the same period, states, 'The Virgin Mary and her sisters merely served by their rare purity to emphasize the grossness of the type, of women in general; they were the pure exceptions who proved the filthy rule'.[2] Clements and Gibaldi, in their study of the novella, argue that the sixteenth-century view of women contained in this form included the belief that they were typically shrewish, deceitful and sexually promiscuous, and could best be controlled by frequent beating. This attitude only begins to change, they suggest, when women themselves produce novellas, 'metamorphosing the once predominantly misogynistic genre into a vehicle for propounding their own strongly feminist ideas'.[3] Latt, considering the English literature of the seventeenth century, has pointed out that 'women most often appear either *as models of generalized virtue* or as examples of the feminine roles of daughter, wife, and mother. *When women are not shown in a domestic context, they are presented as models for men as well as for women'*. This is an interesting claim, as there is little evidence of women appearing as models for both sexes in eighteenth-century fiction; as noted previously, Watt specifically mentions the separation of male and female roles in the literature of the period. Regardless of the rhetoric of authors such as Richardson, the idealised women of the eighteenth-century novel constitute a model for women, not for both sexes.

Latt goes on to point out that, in the seventeenth century, 'Orthodox religious thought maintained that women were intellectually inferior to men and had *a greater carnal susceptibility'*.[4] Women were still considered to be intellectually inferior in the eighteenth century (although this dogma was weakened throughout the period) but, in contrast to their portrayal in previous literature, they were also – as Watt argues – thought to be *less* subject to sexual desire than men. This indicates a major reversal in the imagery applied to the respective sexes. There can be no question that the portrayal of women in eighteenth-century English literature differed markedly from that found in most previous English literature. It is also worth mentioning that there is even a contrast between eighteenth-century literature prior to Richardson, and that produced during and after his adult lifetime. Defoe's Moll and Roxana, for example, were particularised versions of the older female stereotypes, bearing little resemblance to the heroines who were to follow. Richardson's part in remodelling the literary image of women, and the subsequent influence this had on prose-fiction, cannot be too strongly emphasised. Although the post-Richardson heroines of the eighteenth-century novel differ from their predecessors, they do not vary greatly one from another. There *are* differences, but these are outweighed by noticeable similarities.

At this point we can briefly assess the salient issues peculiar to women in the novels discussed. *Pamela* extends the possibility of physical chastity, moral excellence, and socio-economic advancement to a wider range of women. *David Simple* lists injustices against women – particularly those arising from economic dependence – such as parental pressure upon spinsters to force them into economically-oriented marriages. *Amelia* offers an alternative conception of female innocence and moral worth to that proposed by Richardson, attacks (especially female) adultery, and also somewhat undermines the idea that a good woman cannot marry a social inferior. Henry Fielding viewed lapses of physical chastity in a rather more sympathetic manner than many of the other novelists. With *The Vicar of Wakefield*, we find the most extreme emphasis upon physical chastity, coupled with near-misogyny related to allegedly feminine ideas, attitudes, and actions.

The Spiritual Quixote presents a heroine who is subject to jealousy (and is thus more realistic than many of the others), but also contains a blatant attack upon female economic independence, and upon divorce initiated by women. *Evelina* includes the notion of a common standard of behaviour for both men and women (and indeed, the hero, Lord Orville, adheres to a code as rigorous as that subscribed to by the heroine), but the idea is not consistently applied. Additionally, Burney outlines three types of male conduct towards women (thus avoiding the simplistic good/bad model), and indicates to the reader which one she prefers. Caroline, in *Hermsprong*, differs from the other heroines insofar as she is greatly concerned with filial duty (and, unlike Pamela, acts upon it), and rejects the flattery of the hero. Other heroines – such as Evelina – may be sceptical of flattery from dubious characters, but they typically thirst for hyperbole from heroes. Bage's Miss Fluart is by far the most original character in the works examined here: she is as resourceful as Roxana, but with neither the lax morals nor the selfish calculation of the latter. She is prepared to challenge men both intellectually and physically, and thus displays qualities which all of the other writers would have considered too 'masculine' to be appropriate for a woman.

Clearly, there is no unbroken progress from *Pamela* to *Hermsprong*, as far as support for female emancipation is concerned. The novel which occupies the mid-way point historically, *The Vicar of Wakefield*, is completely antithetical to any serious examination of women and the issues relating particularly to them. It also propounds extraordinarily harsh criteria for judging them, outdoing even Richardson's *Pamela*. The authors tended to support the view that women should be confined to the domestic sphere and the realm of morality. With the partial exception of Henry Fielding they welcomed – with some reservations – an increase in educational opportunity for women, but all implied that women are somehow inferior to men, and thus sought to justify the subjugation of women. With the exception of Sarah Fielding, our authors argued – whether tacitly or blatantly – for women to remain economically dependent. Above all, these novelists valued the physical chastity of women very highly, and appear to have agreed that moral excellence – as they saw it – provided sound justification for the exaltation of the individual heroine.

Religion is presented in the novels as a worthy cause, with the Church of England being particularly favoured; apart from Graves, the authors were not religious chauvinists, but it is only in *Hermsprong* that one finds religious pluralism strongly and openly advocated. The primary social function of religion, as it is shown in the novels, is to comfort and pacify the 'lower orders', not least by providing an apology for the wealth and power of their socio-economic superiors. In this way social order could be maintained, 'chaos' and 'anarchy' could be kept at bay, and reform stifled – the very discussion of it being considered an incitement to law-breaking, violence and other assorted evils. The ministers who populate these novels – whether good, like Dr Harrison, or bad, like Dr Blick – argue (with greater or lesser enthusiasm) for the preservation of the status quo as far as the social order is concerned. Harrison, perhaps the most vigorous critic of society to appear in these works, himself only argues for a cleaning-up of some of the corrupt practices illustrated in *Amelia*. Fundamental changes in the distribution of wealth and power played no greater part in the thinking of our fictional clergymen than they did in the thoughts and actions of actual eighteenth-century ministers. The widespread fear of social disruption which haunted the ruling class in the period was much exploited by the Church, whose representatives constantly repeated the claim that any weakening of the Church would eventually lead to complete social collapse – that is to a restructuring of social relations which would not be beneficial to the ruling class and its allies. Therefore, the part played by the Anglican Church and its functionaries in maintaining social order in fact, was to some extent reproduced fictitiously in eighteenth-century novels, by writers sympathetic to the institution.

As indicated above, the main concession which our authors were prepared to make regarding the status quo was the incorporation of individual working and (more frequently) middle-class women into the ranks of their social superiors. Apart from this, social mobility was not endorsed in the novels: in Graves's work even geographical mobility was condemned. His character, Greville, wished to confine agricultural and handicraft workers to the rural areas, regardless of their desires or needs. He does not mention the fact that it was the hardship and poverty characteristic of many such areas which drove workers into the towns, seeking more lucrative employment and being fully prepared to risk the taint of urban 'vice' which all of the authors attack in their works.

The oft-repeated warnings against the towns, and the ideological contrast between an idyllic countryside and the evil and squalid cities, itself indicates the antagonism of our writers to some of the changes taking place in the period. Far from being uncritical exponents of specifically-bourgeois ideas, against the corruption of an entrenched *ancien régime*, these authors – although somewhat influenced by the doctrine of individualism – certainly did not represent the vanguard of bourgeois thought in the century.

As we have seen, Tawney argued that the organic conception of social relations had been replaced by individualism as early as the middle of the seventeenth century; whether or not our novelists believed in the organic view, they definitely promoted a version of it (albeit with concessions to individualism) in their fiction. Moreover, the framework within which they worked was one of class compromise and incorporation, not conflict, or even the dogged pursuit of rational self-interest as against altruism. The incorporation of worthy individuals allegedly built bridges between the classes, and clearly did not foster competition and hostility between them. This approach on the part of the novelists may well have been

related to the comparative weakness and fragmentation of the bourgeoisie during the eighteenth century: they were neither confident
nor powerful enough to seriously challenge the ruling class at this
point. It may be argued that this is precisely why they were content
to accept the existing order, avail themselves of such (social, political, and economic) opportunities as did exist, and to promote class
harmony as being in their own best interests.[5] The most significant
developments relating to an increase in bourgeois power did not
occur until the following century, and therefore the demands and
aims of the eighteenth-century middle class remained fairly modest.
The more radical stance associated with a small number of this class
makes only a fleeting appearance in the novels under consideration,
and then only in *Hermsprong*.

The mainstay of bourgeois criticism of the ruling class to be found
in the novels is, as noted previously, the alleged lechery of men from
the quality. Every author in this study made a nod in the direction of
this convention. But 'convention' is exactly what such criticism had
become, and this sort of attack on the élite features as much in *Pamela*
as it does in *Hermsprong*, the latter being written 55 years (and two
major revolutions – American and French) later. Although the power,
confidence, and political potential of the bourgeoisie did develop
during the period, the writers continued to support the doctrine of
social deference, harmony, compromise, and incorporation. To this
end they created prose-fiction which upheld the status quo, and
provided vindications for the vested interests of those who enjoyed
political and economic power at the expense of the vast majority of
English people.

When one considers the underlying similarities found in the novels, bearing in mind the difference in the quality of writing, the
diverse personal situations of the authors, and the fact that the
works span a period of nearly 60 years, the homogeneity of both
content and authorial assessment appears quite significant. Factors
such as a writer's social origins, and even the actual literary form of
a work are, in this context, secondary issues; the content of the
novels seems to provide a more relevant starting-point from which
the student who views literature as a dialectical or interactive component of literate societies can proceed. Crude estimates of the class-
character of a piece of prose-fiction, which insist upon the sole
priority of a writer's social origins, have never enjoyed much popularity, and have never been convincing: they merely provide some of
the material from which critics such as Spearman can – in true

'Popperian' fashion – assemble straw men which can then be mercilessly torn to shreds.[6]

Critics must always recognise the existence of significant differences between their own society and others, past and present. Nevertheless, interpretation remains a procedure whereby we seek to understand something about other rational beings, however different their social and intellectual capabilities may be. We share with past peoples the task of interpreting reality, regardless of any intellectual or technological advances, and we necessarily employ the same form of reasoning characteristic of any rational being. Literature does not arise from, or develop within, a vacuum of 'art' or 'culture'. Its connections to the wider society are many and complex, quite apart from the position of the individual artist. Therefore, any textual reading must take into account the socio-historical background of the art-work. An understanding of the text necessarily involves an understanding of the context. Such an approach does not necessarily lead to an all-encompassing theory of literature, but it can be applied to the literature of any period, locale or culture. Here, it has been used in an attempt to further understand the eighteenth-century English novel.

Notes

1: LITERATURE AND IDEOLOGY

1. R. Miliband, *Marxism and Politics*, Marxist Introductions (Oxford, 1977), p. 32.
2. This is not the case with every political ideology, but it applies in modern industrial societies particularly where those who seek power claim to be democratic or representative.
3. K. Marx and F. Engels, *The German Ideology*, edited by C. J. Arthur (London, 1974), p. 64.
4. See D. Laurenson and A. Swingewood, *The Sociology of Literature* (London, 1972), and A. S. Collins, *Authorship in the Days of Johnson* (London, 1927), for discussions of patronage and the book trade.
5. I. Watt, *The Rise of the Novel* (Harmondsworth, 1977), p. 55.
6. For useful information on religious tracts from the seventeenth to nineteenth centuries see V. E. Neuburg, *Popular Literature* (Harmondsworth, 1977), pp. 249–64.
7. See, for example, Exodus 21–23 and Deuteronomy 12–26.
8. M. Weber, *The Protestant Ethic and the Spirit of Capitalism*, translated by T. Parsons (London, 1974).
9. R. H. Tawney, *Religion and the Rise of Capitalism* (Harmondsworth, 1977), p. 183.
10. I. Mészáros, *Marx's Theory of Alienation* (London, 1972), p. 225.
11. Ibid., p. 257.
12. Tawney, op. cit., p. 192.
13. C. B. Macpherson, *The Political Theory of Possessive Individualism* (Oxford, 1962), p. 3.
14. Ibid., p. 3.
15. Ibid., p. 215.
16. Ibid., p. 219.
17. Ibid., p. 220.
18. Ibid., pp. 222, 223, 224.
19. Ibid., p. 221.
20. L. Stone, *The Family, Sex and Marriage in England 1500–1800* (Harmondsworth, 1979), p. 178.
21. K. Marx, *Introduction to a Critique of Political Economy*, included in K. Marx and F. Engels, op. cit., p. 124.
22. S. Avineri, *The Social and Political Thought of Karl Marx* (Cambridge, 1968), p. 95.
23. Watt, op. cit., p. 102, points out that the influential philosopher, Hume, was not a supporter of individualism; this may have helped to discourage some authors from the extreme individualism found in Defoe.
24. Ibid., pp. 66–103.
25. See Laurenson and Swingewood, op. cit., pp. 175–206, for a consideration of Fielding's attitude towards the social changes then occurring.

26.   M. D. George, *London Life in the Eighteenth Century* (Harmondsworth, 1966), p. 159.
27.   Stone, op. cit., p. 232.
28.   A. Adburgham, *Women in Print* (London, 1972), p. 56.
29.   Stone (1979), op. cit., p. 233.
30.   M. LeGates, 'The Cult of Womanhood in Eighteenth-Century Thought', *Eighteenth-Century Studies*, 10, (1976–7), pp. 21–39, (p. 37).
31.   S. C. Carpenter, *Eighteenth-Century Church and People* (London, 1959), p. 184.

2: THE NOVEL AND SOCIETY: 1740–1800

1.   I. Watt, *The Rise of the Novel* (Harmondsworth, 1977), pp. 14–15.
2.   Ibid., p. 13.
3.   Ibid., p. 14.
4.   Ibid., p. 14.
5.   Ibid., pp. 16, 19, 20, 33.
6.   Ibid., p. 12; emphasis added.
7.   Ibid., p. 34.
8.   Ibid., pp. 16, 13.
9.   Ibid., p. 30.
10.   J. M. S. Tompkins, *The Popular Novel in England 1770–1800* (London, 1932), pp. 70, 71.
11.   W. Benjamin, *Illuminations* (London, 1977), p. 86.
12.   R. Williams, *The Long Revolution* (Harmondsworth, 1965), pp. 257–61. See chapter 5 for the basis of Williams's sample.
13.   T. C. D. Eaves and B. D. Kimpel, *Samuel Richardson: A Biography* (Oxford, 1971), pp. 2, 3–4. See also, W. Scott, *Lives of the Novelists* (Oxford, 1906), p. 209.
14.   P. Rogers, *Henry Fielding: A Biography* (London, 1979), p. 14.
15.   C. J. Hill, 'The Literary Career of Richard Graves's, *Smith College Studies in Modern Languages*, XVI, October 1934 – July 1935, pp. 1–148, (p. 2).
16.   See A. Lytton Sells, *Oliver Goldsmith: His Life and Works* (London, 1974), p. 24, and R. M. Wardle, *Oliver Goldsmith* (Lawrence, Kansas, 1957), pp. 39–40.
17.   A. Dobson, *Fanny Burney* (London, 1903), pp. 5, 7.
18.   W. Scott, *Lives of the Novelists* (Oxford, 1906), pp. 259, 253.
19.   R. Williams, op. cit., p. 182.
20.   Watt, op. cit., pp. 52–3.
21.   Ibid., p. 39. See also, F. W. J. Hemmings, 'Realism and the Novel: The Eighteenth-Century Beginnings', in F. W. J. Hemmings (ed.) *The Age of Realism*, (Harmondsworth, 1974), p. 16, and R. Williams, op. cit., p. 182.
22.   Watt, op. cit., pp. 39, 45.
23.   Ibid., p. 46.
24.   Hemmings, op. cit., p. 16.
25.   R. Williams, op. cit., p. 184.

26. Watt, op. cit., p. 65.
27. S. Richardson, *Pamela*, Everyman's Library, 2 volumes (London, 1914), vol. 2, p. v.
28. Ibid., vol. 1, pp. 76–82, 450–3. All further quotations from vol. 1 unless otherwise stated.
29. Eaves and Kimpel, op. cit., p. 100.
30. J. Boswell, *The Life of Johnson*, The Penguin English Library (Harmondsworth, 1979), p. 159; emphasis added.
31. Tompkins, op. cit., p. 71.
32. H. Fielding in his preface to S. Fielding, *The Adventures of David Simple*, edited with an introduction by M. Kelsall, Oxford English Novels (London, 1969), p. 5.
33. Ibid., Kelsall, p. xii.
34. Ibid., H. Fielding, p. 7.
35. Ibid., Kelsall, p. xii.
36. Ibid., H. Fielding, p. 7.
37. J. Collier, preface to *Volume the Last*, included in S. Fielding, op. cit., p. 311. See Kelsall's note to p. 309, on p. 435.
38. Ibid., Collier, p. 311.
39. H. Fielding, *Amelia*, Everyman's Library, 2 volumes bound together (London, 1974), p. x. All reference to vol. 1 unless otherwise stated.
40. Ibid., p. 3.
41. Ibid., p. 4; emphasis added.
42. Ibid., vol. 2, p. 312.
43. R. Alter, 'Fielding's Problem Novel', in C. Rawson, (ed.) *Henry Fielding*, Penguin Critical Anthologies (Harmondsworth, 1973), pp. 555–86, (p. 558).
44. G. B. Needham and R. P. Utter, *Pamela's Daughters* (London, 1937), p. 19.
45. R. Graves, *The Spiritual Quixote*, edited with an introduction by C. Tracy, Oxford English Novels (London, 1967), p. 3.
46. Ibid., p. 3.
47. Ibid., p. 6.
48. Ibid., p. 9.
49. Ibid., Tracy, p. xx.
50. Ibid., Graves, pp. 187–223.
51. O. Goldsmith, *The Vicar of Wakefield*, Everyman's Library (London, 1908), All references to this edition unless otherwise stated.
52. G. D. Carnall in J. Butt, *English Literature in the Mid-Eighteenth Century*, edited and completed by G. D. Carnall, *Oxford History of English Literature*, 13 volumes (London, 1979), vol. 8, p. 475.
53. Wardle, op. cit., p. 169.
54. Lytton Sells, op. cit., p. 213.
55. Ibid., p. 280.
56. W. Allen, *The English Novel* (Harmondsworth, 1958), p. 95.
57. A. Friedman in his introduction to O. Goldsmith, *The Vicar of Wakefield*, Oxford English Novels (London, 1974), p. viii.
58. F. Burney, *Evelina*, edited with an introduction by E. A. Bloom, Oxford English Novels (London, 1968), p. 7.

59. Ibid., p. 8.
60. Ibid., p. 9.
61. Ibid., p. xliii.
62. P. M. Spacks, *Imagining a Self* (Cambridge, Massachusetts, 1976), p. 176.
63. Allen, op. cit., p. 95.
64. Spacks, op. cit., p. 176.
65. Ibid., p. 160.
66. Tompkins, op. cit., p. 198.
67. Ibid., p. 198.
68. Allen, op. cit., p. 102.
69. R. Bage, *Hermsprong, or Man as He is Not*, with an introduction by V. Wilkins (London, 1951), pp. 15, 53, 246.
70. Allen, op. cit., p. 102.

3: SAMUEL RICHARDSON: *PAMELA* (1740)

1. S. Richardson, *Pamela*, Everyman's Library, 2 volumes (London, 1914), vol. 1, pp. 22, 26–7.
2. Ibid., p. 124.
3. Ibid., p. 166.
4. Ibid., p. 175.
5. Ibid., p. 264.
6. Ibid., p. 75.
7. Ibid., p. 56.
8. Ibid., p. 83.
9. Ibid., pp. 168, 355.
10. M. Walzer, *The Revolution of the Saints* (New York, 1968), p. 216.
11. Richardson, op. cit., p. 234.
12. Ibid., p. 427.
13. Ibid., pp. 215, 229.
14. Ibid., p. 230. Note Richardson's use of the 'chain of being' analogy here – that notion contrasted sharply with the atomistic individualism which became influential in the period.
15. Ibid., vol. 2, p. 168.
16. Ibid., pp. 12, 23, 41.
17. Ibid., pp. 189, 193.
18. T. Eagleton, *The Rape of Clarissa* (Minneapolis, 1986), p. 37; I. Watt, *The Rise of the Novel* (Harmondsworth, 1977), p. 187.
19. Richardson, op. cit., pp. 320–2.
20. Ibid., p. 233. Pamela claims that her main concern is to protect B. from 'rude jests'.
21. P. M. Spacks, *Imagining a Self* (Cambridge, Massachusetts, 1976), p. 197.
22. Richardson, op. cit., p. 57.
23. See B. Kriessman, *Pamela-Shamela*, University of Nebraska Studies: New Series 22 (Lincoln, Nebraska, 1960), for a survey of responses to *Pamela*.

24. Spacks, op. cit., p. 213.
25. Richardson, op. cit., p. 395.
26. K. Rogers, 'Richardson's Empathy with Women', in A. Diamond and L. R. Edwards (eds), *The Authority of Experience: Essays in Feminist Criticism* (Amherst, Massachusetts, 1977), pp. 118–36, (p. 119).
27. Richardson, op. cit., pp. 406–9.
28. I. Konigsberg, *Samuel Richardson and the Dramatic Novel* (Lexington, Kentucky, 1968), p. 17.
29. Stone, (1979), op. cit., pp. 329–30.
30. Eagleton, op. cit., p. 36.
31. Kriessman, op. cit., contains 'Anti-Pamelist' arguments from Richardson's contemporaries which specifically attack the *laxity* of his moral outlook.
32. Walzer, op. cit., p. 193.
33. Richardson, op. cit., p. 302.
34. Walzer, op. cit., p. 193.
35. Richardson, op. cit., p. 4.
36. D. L. Ball, *Samuel Richardson's Theory of Fiction* (The Hague, 1971), p. 253.
37. Richardson, op. cit., p. 214, 401–2.
38. Ibid., see especially vol. 2, pp. 392–3.
39. Ibid., pp. 412–13.
40. For useful material regarding Puritan diaries and journals see O. C. Watkins, *The Puritan Experience* (London, 1972).
41. Ibid., pp. 18–24.
42. Richardson, op. cit., p. 44.
43. Spacks, op. cit., p. 8.
44. Critics often argue that Richardson was opposed to the 'double standard', particularly in the light of his later work, *Sir Charles Grandison*. K. Rogers, op. cit., p. 119, in her attempt to glorify Richardson at Fielding's expense, raises no objections to the former's complacency here, yet asserts that Fielding's opposition to the double standard 'was not very convincing'.
45. Richardson, op. cit., p. 451.
46. Richardson was probably influenced by the criticism that his was a pragmatic and calculating view of morality – he ensured that *Clarissa* could not be subjected to the same attack.
47. Watt, op. cit., pp. 159, 150.
48. Ibid., pp. 183–5.
49. All 'respectable' women would be assumed to support moral endeavour.
50. Watt, op. cit., p. 185.
51. Ibid., p. 181.
52. Ibid., p. 182.
53. K. Rogers, op. cit., p. 135.
54. Writers during this period considered 'example' to be very important, as shown by their frequent stress upon, for instance, they way in which an employer's behaviour could determine the conduct of servants and others. As noted above, Richardson did not think that women

were *typically* highly virtuous, but rather believed that they *could be* if
they acted in accordance with a strict code of conduct specifically
designed for them. One literary consequence of this is that Richardson
tried to represent Pamela as being both a 'natural' or 'realistic' character, whilst at the same time being a woman who had attained –
morally – as much as any woman might hope to achieve. *Pamela*
purports to show how a woman from a humble background can excel
if she strives for what the author himself believed to be a standard of
conduct seldom found anywhere in his society, and even less often
amongst women of Pamela's class.

55. Richardson in J. Carroll (ed.), *Selected Letters of Samuel Richardson*
(Oxford, 1964), pp. 202, 203, 162. Note that Richardson here mentions
childbirth and its pain as another part of the 'punishment'.
56. M. Kinkead-Weekes, *Samuel Richardson, Dramatic Novelist* (London,
1973), p. 63. K. Rogers, op. cit., p. 119, deems Richardson a 'radical
feminist' – an absurd proposition, in my view.
57. I know of no interest peculiar to women that Richardson supported.
K. Rogers, ibid., p. 119, imagines that the author thought of marriage
as 'a partnership between equals', but all of the evidence refutes this
claim.
58. Richardson in Carroll, op. cit., p. 178. This flatly contradicts K. Rogers,
op. cit., p. 132, who claims that he 'did not glorify domestic pursuits'.
59. Richardson, op. cit., pp. 260–1.
60. Ibid., p. 57.
61. Ibid., p. 93.
62. Ibid., pp. 157, 174, 179.
63. Ibid., p. 218.
64. Ibid., pp. 244, 437–8.
65. Ibid., pp. 24, 44, 45, 159.
66. Ibid., pp. 143, 162.
67. Ibid., p. 205.
68. Ibid., pp. 239, 314, 394.
69. Ibid., pp. 435–41.
70. Ibid., p. 308.
71. Ibid., p. 331. For Pamela's codification of B.'s rules see pp. 406–9.
72. Ibid., p. 316.

4: SARAH FIELDING: *DAVID SIMPLE* (1744)

1. R. Alter, 'Fielding's Problem Novel', in C. Rawson (ed.), *Henry Fielding*, Penguin Critical Anthologies (Harmondsworth, 1973), pp. 555–86
(p. 560).
2. J. Mullan, *Sentiment and Sociability* (Oxford, 1988), p. 34.
3. S. Fielding, *The Adventures of David Simple*, edited with an introduction
by M. Kelsall, Oxford English Novels (London, 1969), pp. 249–50.
4. Ibid., p. 285.
5. Ibid., p. 134.
6. Ibid., pp. 33–4.

7. Ibid., p. 176.
8. Ibid., p. 180.
9. Ibid., p. 178.
10. Ibid., pp. 179, 182.
11. Ibid., pp. 286, 280.
12. Ibid., p. 248.
13. Ibid., p. 285.
14. Ibid., pp. 32, 52, 64.
15. Ibid., p. 86.
16. Ibid., p. 101.
17. Ibid., pp. 129–30.
18. Ibid., pp. 99–100.
19. Ibid., p. 113.
20. Ibid., p. 169.
21. Ibid., p. 167. Although Camilla has some brief experience of begging.
22. Ibid., pp. 108–9, 151, 200, 181.
23. Ibid., pp. 191, 254.
24. Ibid., p. 35 and p. 114; p. 36 and p. 46; pp. 45, 65, 142, 271.
25. G. B. Needham and R. P. Utter, *Pamela's Daughters* (London, 1937), *passim*.
26. Mullan, op. cit., p. 13.
27. S. Fielding, op. cit., p. 146.
28. Ibid., pp. 12, 19, 146; pp. 171, 288.
29. Ibid., pp. 77–81, 118, 279, 300.
30. Ibid., p. 189.
31. Ibid., pp. 63, 252.
32. Ibid., pp. 167–8.
33. Ibid., p. 251.
34. Ibid., pp. 304–5, (p. 304).
35. Ibid., p. 304.
36. Ibid., p. 304.
37. Mullan, op. cit., p. 123. Mullan is here discussing Mackenzie but I think his point applies to *David Simple*.
38. S. Fielding, op. cit., p. 314.

5: HENRY FIELDING: *AMELIA* (1751)

1. J. Cleland's review of *Amelia* in C. Rawson (ed.), *Henry Fielding*, Penguin Critical Anthologies (Harmondsworth, 1973), pp. 120–1, (p. 121).
2. H. R. Steeves, *Before Jane Austen* (London, 1966), p. 125.
3. K. Rogers, 'Richardson's Empathy with Women', in A. Diamond and L. R. Edwards (eds), *The Authority of Experience*: Essays in *Feminist Criticism* (Massachusetts, 1977), pp. 118–36, (p. 119). As noted in Chapter 3, this writer compares Fielding unfavourably to Richardson, seeing the former's work as 'conditioned by the antifeminist prejudice of his time', and deeming the latter a 'radical feminist'. For a very different feminist view of Fielding see A. J. Smallwood, *Fielding and the Woman Question* (New York, 1989). Smallwood writes, 'Fielding's portrayal of

  Amelia is a resounding affirmation of wifely self-sacrifice, not out of
any masculine complacency on Fielding's part, but because it en-
shrines the values of friendship which Fielding would extend to human relationships of all kinds throughout society'. Smallwood, op.
cit., p. 168.

4. H. Fielding, *Amelia*, Everyman's Library (London, 1974), p. 62. All
references to vol. 1 unless otherwise stated.

5. R. Alter, 'Fielding's Problem Novel', in Rawson, op. cit., pp. 555–86,
(p. 573). Interestingly, Amelia is not a beauty and even suffers some
disfigurement of her nose – something which Fielding's critics found
most amusing.

6. See R. Paulson, *Satire and the Novel in Eighteenth-Century England* (New
Haven, Connecticut, and London, 1967), p. 113. Paulson points out
that Parson Adams – in *Joseph Andrews* – 'is unable (from simplicity
and goodness) to recognise malice when it appears'. Fielding's conception of innocence was certainly very different to that held by
Richardson.

7. H. Fielding, op. cit., pp. 84, 117.

8. Ibid., vol. 2, p. 310.

9. A. L. Barbauld, from 'Fielding', in Rawson, op. cit., pp. 206–15, (p.
212).

10. Ibid., p. 214.

11. H. Fielding, op. cit., vol. 2, p. 13.

12. Ibid., vol. 2, pp. 166, 186.

13. M. C. Battestin, *The Moral Basis of Fielding's Art* (Middletown, Connecticut, 1959), p. 121. This study provides a discussion of Fielding's
Latitudinarian position.

14. H. Fielding, op. cit., vol. 2, p. 187.

15. Watt, op. cit., p. 183. See also p. 158 n. 46, below.

16. H. Fielding, op. cit., vol. 2, p. 278. See J. C. D. Clark, *English Society
1688–1832* (Cambridge, 1985), pp. 93–118 for a discussion of the respective ideals of the Christian and the gentleman; duelling, suggests
Clark, was a phenomenon which illustrated one of the serious contradictions between the two sets of ideals.

17. H. Fielding, op. cit., vol. 2, pp. 278, 279. As Harrison is implicitly
claiming that duelling is 'caused' by women, and that such conduct is
not really 'feminine', it is clear that he defines 'feminine' according to
some ideal of his own – and not according to what he takes to be the
attitudes and actions of real women.

18. Ibid., p. 283.

19. Ibid., vol. 2, p. 97.

20. Ibid., p. 170.

21. Alter in Rawson, op. cit., p. 565.

22. J. A. Work, 'Henry Fielding, Christian Censor', in F. W. Hilles (ed.),
The Age of Johnson (New Haven, Connecticut, Yale, 1949), pp. 139–48,
(p. 144).

23. This is one of countless examples which indicates the folly of viewing
Fielding as a mere libertine.

24. H. Fielding, op. cit., vol. 2, p. 172. The assumption here is that it is the
adultery of married women which constitutes the main problem.

25. G. Rudé, *Hanoverian London* (London, 1971), p. 72.
26. D. Jarrett, *England in the Age of Hogarth* (St Albans, 1976), p. 112.
27. H. Fielding, op. cit., p. 108.
28. Ibid., vol. 2, p. 132.
29. Alter, in Rawson, op. cit., p. 560. See Chapter 6 below for a fuller discussion of 'human nature'.
30. H. Fielding, op. cit., vol. 2, p. 159.
31. Ibid., p. 9.
32. Ibid., vol. 2, p. 107.
33. Ibid., vol. 2, p. 131; emphasis added.
34. Ibid., vol. 2, p. 228.
35. Ibid., vol. 2, p. 229.
36. Ibid., vol. 2, p. 229.
37. Ibid., vol. 2, p. 230.
38. Ibid., p. 241.
39. Ibid., p. 125.
40. Ibid., vol. 2, p. 304.
41. Ibid., vol. 2, p. 49; emphasis added.
42. Ibid., vol. 2, pp. 25–6; emphasis added.
43. Ibid., vol. 2, p. 50.
44. I. Watt, *The Rise of the Novel* (Harmondsworth, 1977), pp. 185–6.
45. Cross-class marriages were frowned upon by many eighteenth-century commentators (even when a *man* of some status married downwards); Fielding himself suffered derision when he made such a marriage, which is ironic given that he had earlier attacked Richardson (in *Shamela*) for encouraging unequal matches.
46. H. Fielding, op. cit., vol. 2, p. 50.
47. Ibid., vol. 2, p. 134.
48. Ibid., vol. 2, p. 150.
49. Ibid., vol. 2, p. 50. We believe Amelia whilst we may doubt the similar claim made by Pamela.
50. Ibid., vol. 2, p. 304.
51. M. Price, 'Fielding: The Comedy of Forms', in Rawson, op. cit., pp. 395–423, (p. 415).

6: OLIVER GOLDSMITH: THE VICAR OF WAKEFIELD (1766)

1. Compare R. H. Hopkins, *The True Genius of Oliver Goldsmith* (Baltimore, 1969), and S. Bäckman, *This Singular Tale*, (Berlingska Bocktryckeviet, Lund, 1971). See also J. Mullan, *Sentiment and Sociability* (Oxford, 1988), p. 139; as he suggests, 'If *The Vicar of Wakefield* was a parody, it was, and is, difficult to distinguish it from the type that it might have parodied'.
2. As Hopkins points out, the Vicar tends to see his children in a somewhat 'economic' light, Hopkins, op. cit., p. 186.
3. O. Goldsmith, *The Vicar of Wakefield*, Everyman's Library (London, 1908), p. 6.
4. Ibid., p. 7. I believe that one of Goldsmith's aims is to show that the disasters which occur stem from the fact that Primrose neglects his

duty regarding the control of his wife and children; he seems to be suggesting that the Vicar is simply not strict enough in this respect.

5.   Ibid., p. 18.
6.   Ibid., p. 20.
7.   Ibid., p. 24.
8.   Ibid., p. 26.
9.   Ibid., p. 24.
10. Ibid., p. 35.
11. Ibid., p. 44.
12. Ibid., p. 46. The 'ladies' are actually whores.
13. Ibid., p. 47.
14. Ibid., p. 58.
15. Ibid., p. 66.
16. Ibid., p. 66.
17. Ibid., p. 96.
18. Ibid., p. 97; emphasis added.
19. Ibid., p. 145.
20. Ibid., p. 147.
21. Ibid., p. 154.
22. Ibid., p. 158.
23. Ibid., pp. 195–6; emphasis added.
24. Ibid., p. 216.
25. Ibid., p. 214.
26. Bäckman, op. cit., holds this sort of view.
27. W. Allen, *The English Novel* (Harmondsworth, 1958), p. 82.
28. A. Lytton Sells, Oliver Goldsmith: His Life and Works (London, 1974), p. 266.
29. Goldsmith, op. cit., pp. 11–12.
30. Ibid., p. 188.
31. Ibid., pp. 20, 23.
32. Ibid., p. 36. Of course if opinions are formed *involuntarily* it makes no sense to speak of negligence or corruption in this context.
33. Ibid., p. 106.
34. Ibid., p. 107.
35. Ibid., pp. 106–7.
36. Ibid., p. 107.
37. Ibid., p. 108.
38. Ibid., p. 109; emphasis added.
39. Ibid., p. 109.
40. Ibid., p. 109.
41. Ibid., p. 110.
42. Ibid., p. 158.
43. The more active strand of individualism had (more or less) shed its religious trappings by this time; in its secular form it appeared as the bourgeois doctrine of economic individualism.
44. Ibid., p. 160.
45. Ibid., p. 163.
46. Ibid., p. 166.
47. Ibid., p. 170.

Notes to Chapter 7

48.   Ibid., pp. 172–3; emphasis added. As Mullan suggests, there may be some satire intended here, 'But this was too close to current ideology to look very odd to its polite readers'. Mullan, op. cit., p. 145.
49.   I. Mészáros, Marx's Theory of Alienation (London, 1972), p. 166.
50.   Goldsmith, op. cit., p. 174.
51.   Ibid., p. 175.
52.   Ibid., p. 188.
53.   Ibid., p. 189.
54.   Ibid., p. 190.
55.   Ibid., p. 190. It is worth comparing this with an argument put by William Paley: 'If in comparing the different conditions of social life we bring religion into the account, the argument is still easier. Religion smooths all inequalities because it unfolds a prospect which makes all earthly distinctions nothing'. Quoted in J. C. D. Clark, *English Society 1688–1832* (Cambridge, 1985), p. 262. Clark disapprovingly notes that 'radical historians' often deride such apologies for inequality.

7: RICHARD GRAVES: THE SPIRITUAL QUIXOTE (1773)

1.   R. Graves, edited with an introduction by C. Tracy, Oxford English Novels (London, 1967), p. 19; emphasis added.
2.   Ibid., p. 20; emphasis added.
3.   Ibid., pp. 21, 22, 23.
4.   Ibid., p. 26.
5.   Ibid., p. 27.
6.   Ibid., p. 30.
7.   Ibid., p. 49.
8.   Ibid., p. 76; emphasis added.
9.   Ibid., p. 227.
10.   Ibid., pp. 378, 428.
11.   Ibid., p. 446.
12.   Ibid., pp. 154–5. The 'quixote' convention necessitates the hero being deluded, but Graves is doing more than simply following a literary convention – the work is intended as an attack on Methodism at least as much as it is meant to be an entertainment.
13.   Ibid., pp. 32, 38.
14.   Ibid., pp. 45, 62.
15.   Ibid., p. 114. This is supposed to be a function of (a) working-class ignorance and (b) Methodist jargon.
16.   Ibid., p. 146.
17.   Ibid., p. 269.
18.   Ibid., p. 40; emphasis added.
19.   A. D. Gilbert, *Religion and Society in Industrial England: Church, Chapel and Social Change* (London, 1976), p. 27.
20.   Graves, op. cit., p. 128; emphasis added.
21.   On this point it might be argued that the Methodists held a more specifically 'Protestant' position than the Anglicans.

22. Graves, op. cit., p. 350.
23. Ibid., p. 432; first and fourth emphasis added.
24. Ibid., p. 449. It is a good job for Graves and other Anglicans that the Established Church was not required to demonstrate the righteousness of its own doctrines and practices by 'visible proof'.
25. Ibid., p. 450.
26. Ibid., p. 452.
27. Ibid., pp. 450–1; second emphasis added.
28. Ibid., p. 451.
29. Ibid.
30. J. Cannon, *Aristocratic Century: the Peerage of Eighteenth-Century England*, (Cambridge, 1984), p. 153.
31. R. E. Davies, *Methodism* (Harmondsworth, Pelican 1964), p. 84; emphasis added.
32. Ibid., p. 76; emphasis added.
33. A. Armstrong, *The Church of England, the Methodists and Society 1700–1850* (London, 1973), p. 103.
34. Gilbert, op. cit., p. 19.
35. J. C. D. Clark, *English Society 1688–1832* (Cambridge, 1985), p. 235.
36. T. B. Shepherd, *Methodism and the Literature of the Eighteenth Century* (London, 1940), p. 215.
37. Ibid., p. 213.
38. Ibid., p. 216.
39. Ibid., p. 220. In Shepherd's account, Smollett's *Humphry Clinker* is 'as much an apologia for Methodism as it is a criticism'! See Shepherd, p. 224.
40. C. J. Hill, 'The Literary Career of Richard Graves', Smith College Studies in Modern Languages, XVI, October 1934 – July 1935, pp. 1–148 (p. 16).
41. Apart from Graves's paragons (Ophelia, Charlotte and Isabella) and his 'wicked' women (Widow Townsend, Mrs Skelton, Lady Ruelle and Charlotte's stepmother), there are a number of female characters left over who do not fit into either category. One might also argue that Julia is one of the most realistic heroines in the eighteenth-century English novel.
42. Graves, op. cit., pp. 78, 80–2, 87–96.
43. Ibid., p. 99.
44. Ibid., pp. 237, 238.
45. Ibid., pp. 239–40.
46. Ibid., p. 432. See G. B. Needham and R. P. Utter, *Pamela's Daughters* (London, 1937), pp. 140–64, for a full discussion of fainting and its significance in the English novel. See also J. Mullan, *Sentiment and Sociability* (London, 1988), pp. 201–40 for the connection between feeling and its bodily manifestations.
47. According to C. J. Hill, Charlotte Rivers (née Woodville) is modelled upon Graves's own wife, and the whole story of Mr Rivers is almost certainly autobiographical, as is that of Ophelia and Mr Graham. See C. J. Hill, op. cit., p. 132 and, for a detailed account of the parallels between Graves's life and the content of his novel, see pp. 61—71.

48. Graves, op. cit., p. 188, emphasis added; pp. 190, 194.
49. Ibid., p. 200.
50. Ibid., pp. 217, 218, 203, 222.
51. Graves was certainly concerned to make an apology for what were regarded as imprudent matches; both his relationship with Utrecia Smith, whom he jilted, and his later marriage to Lucy Bartholomew were assessed as such by his contemporaries. See C. J. Hill, op. cit., pp. 61–71.
52. Graves, op. cit., pp. 149–57. See also C. J. Hill, op. cit., p. 124.
53. Graves, op. cit., pp. 145, 148, 173.
54. Ibid., p. 154; second emphasis added.
55. Ibid., p. 155; second emphasis added.
56. Ibid., p. 155.
57. Ibid., p. 157.
58. See E. Goffman, *Stigma* (Harmondsworth, 1968), on 'passing'.
59. Graves, op. cit., pp. 69, 70.
60. Ibid., pp. 159, 160, 168.
61. Ibid., pp. 172–3.
62. Ibid., pp. 411–5.
63. Ibid., pp. 61, 185, 341, for examples.
64. Ibid., p. 183.
65. Ibid., p. 310.
66. Ibid., p. 311; emphasis added.
67. K. Marx in D. McLellan (ed.), *Marx's Grundrisse* (St Albans, 1971), p. 89.
68. K. Marx, *Capital*, 3 volumes (London, 1974) vol. 1, p. 667.
69. Graves, op. cit., p. 280.
70. Ibid., pp. 386–7.
71. Ibid., pp. 378–9, 416–23.
72. Ibid., pp. 380–1.
73. Ibid., p. 461.
74. C. J. HIll, op. cit., p. 122.
75. C. Whibley in his introduction to R. Graves, *The Spiritual Quixote*, 2 volumes (London, 1926), vol. 1, pp. xii, xix. Anon, 'Richard Graves', in *Times Literary Supplement*, 11 May 1922, p. 298. C. Tracy in Graves, op. cit., pp. xvii, xvi.
76. M. Rymer, 'Satiric Technique in *The Spiritual Quixote*: Some Comments', *Durham University Journal*, 65, 1972–3, pp. 54–64, (p. 54).
77. C. J. Hill, op. cit., pp. 122–3.
78. Ibid., p. 125.
79. Graves, op. cit., p. 449.

8: FANNY BURNEY: EVELINA (1778)

1. F. Burney, *Evelina*, edited with an introduction by E. A. Bloom, Oxford English Novels (London, 1968), pp. 20, 21.
2. Ibid., p. 108.
3. Ibid., p. 107.

4. Ibid., pp. 111, 275.
5. Ibid., p. 361.
6. Ibid., pp. 19, 28.
7. Ibid., pp. 240, 346, 164.
8. Ibid., p. 109.
9. Ibid., pp. 80, 112, 113.
10. Ibid., pp. 65, 77, 144–50, 116.
11. Ibid., p. 186.
12. Ibid., pp. 221, 223, 224.
13. Ibid., p. 220.
14. Ibid., p. 123.
15. Ibid., pp. 183, 343.
16. Ibid., p. 217; emphasis added.
17. Ibid., p. 261.
18. Ibid., pp. 161, 164.
19. Ibid., p. 164; emphasis added.
20. Ibid., pp. 126–7; emphasis added.
21. Ibid., pp. 379, 387, 406; emphasis added.
22. Ibid., p. 268.
23. Ibid., p. 289.
24. Ibid., p. 217. See E. Goffman, *The Presentation of Self in Everyday Life* (London, 1966).
25. Burney, op. cit., p. 164.
26. See D. Riesman, *The Lonely Crowd* (New York, 1953).
27. Burney, op. cit., p. 148.
28. Ibid., pp. 12, 13, 14.
29. Ibid., p. 94; emphasis added.
30. Ibid., pp. 40–8.
31. Ibid., pp. 97–101, 100, 206.
32. Ibid., p. 171.
33. Ibid., p. 172.
34. Ibid., p. 223.
35. Ibid., p. 83.
36. Ibid., p. 174.
37. Ibid., p. 219.
38. Ibid., p. 248.
39. Ibid., p. 30; emphasis added.
40. Ibid., p. 31.
41. Ibid., pp. 32, 34.
42. Ibid., p. 106; emphasis added.
43. Ibid., p. 106.
44. Ibid., p. 113.
45. G. B. Needham and R. P. Utter, *Pamela's Daughters* (London, 1937), argue that this is a recurring theme in English prose-fiction. It may be that the parallel between this sort of novel and the Cinderella story is even closer than they suggest; the Opie's collection of fairy tales shows that in most of the tales drawn from *Cinderella* the heroine is – like Evelina – not a poor girl but rather one from a noble or royal family. See I. Opie and P. Opie, *The Classic Fairy Tales* (London, 1980), pp. 152–9.

46. Burney, op. cit., p. 18.
47. Ibid., p. 16.
48. Ibid., p. 163.
49. Ibid., p. 338; it is worth noting Villars's use of the anachronistic 'thee', 'thou' and 'thy' (here and below), which is presumably employed to lend seriousness to his utterances.
50. Ibid., p. 405.
51. Ibid., p. 294.

9: ROBERT BAGE: HERMSPRONG (1796)

1. G. Kelly, *The English Jacobin Novel* (London, 1976), pp. 40, 60. P. Faulkner, *Robert Bage* (Boston, 1979), p. 134. P. Faulkner, 'Man as He is Not', *Durham University Journal*, 1964–5, 57, pp. 137–47, (p. 140). V. Wilkins in his introduction to R. Bage, *Hermsprong, or Man as He is Not* (London, 1951), pp. v, viii.
2. Bage, op. cit., pp. 72, 73, 74.
3. Ibid., pp. 69, 101, 105, 106, 184, 190, 215–6, 231.
4. Ibid., p. 246.
5. Ibid., pp. 51–3, 81, 85.
6. Ibid., pp. 86, 91, 103, 104–5.
7. Ibid., pp. 110, 111, 113.
8. Ibid., pp. 189, 210.
9. Ibid., p. 191.
10. Ibid., pp. 211, 212–4, 215.
11. Ibid., p. 247.
12. Ibid., p. x.
13. Ibid., p. 18.
14. Ibid., p. 30.
15. Ibid., p. 27.
16. Ibid., p. 57.
17. Ibid., pp. 65, 67.
18. Ibid., p. 135; emphasis added.
19. Ibid., p. 137; emphasis added.
20. Ibid., pp. 142–3.
21. Ibid., p. 170. Even Bage's use of pseudo-anthropological anecdotes – a device employed in the eighteenth century to criticise European societies and assert cultural relativism – becomes a means of supporting the 'feminine virtues' lauded by conservative thinkers.
22. Ibid., pp. 172–3; emphasis added.
23. L. Stone, *The Family, Sex and Marriage in England 1500–1800* (Harmondsworth, 1979), pp. 415–24.
24. Quoted in ibid., p. 318.
25. Bage, op. cit., pp. 6, 8, 15.
26. Ibid., pp. 98, 168, 148, 14, 67–9, 83, 123–4.
27. Ibid., pp. 45–6, (p. 46).
28. Ibid., p. 44, for a list of Woodcock's virtues; see also p. 239.
29. Ibid., p. 10.
30. Ibid., pp. 14, 46.

31. Ibid., p. 44.
32. Ibid., pp. 14, 45.
33. Ibid., pp. 46, 41.
34. Ibid., pp. 41–2, 42, 43.
35. Ibid., pp. 70, 83, 84. Note Bage's unusual use of 'consuetudinage' here.
36. Ibid., p. 92. For an account of these riots see L. Jewitt (ed.), *The Life of William Hutton* (London, 1872).
37. Bage, op. cit., p. 93.
38. Ibid., pp. 238, 164, 167.
39. Ibid., pp. 12–13.
40. Ibid., p. 21.
41. Ibid., p. 83.
42. P. D. Tripathi, *The Doctrinal English Novel* (Calcutta, 1977), considers Hermsprong to be a portrait of bourgeois 'man', but I think that he perhaps overstates his case.
43. Bage, op. cit., pp. 73, 202.
44. Ibid., pp. 87, 88, 89.
45. Ibid., p. 94.
46. Ibid., pp. 133, 134, 134–5.
47. Ibid., pp. 220–2. The reader only learns of the 'riot' in this indirect manner.
48. Ibid., p. 225.
49. Ibid., p. 219. Protests against eighteenth-century employers were typically related to the cost of living, particularly the cost of food; they were not usually attempts to get a higher standard of living.
50. Anon., Review of Scott's *Lives of the Novelists*, in the *Quarterly Review*, 1826, vol. 34, pp. 349–78, (p. 367).
51. See W. Allen, *The English Novel* (Harmondsworth, 1958), p. 102; Wilkins in Bage, op. cit., p. v.; Faulkner (1964–5), op. cit., p. 143.
52. Kelly, op. cit., pp. 34, 27, 61.
53. Ibid., pp. 29, 27.
54. Of course much of what passes for radical ideas and practices poses little or no threat to the established order – as many conservatives fully appreciate.
55. Tripathi, op. cit., pp. 198, 208.
56. Bage, op. cit., p. 226.
57. Ibid., p. 227.
58. Allen, op. cit., p. 102.
59. G. S. Veitch, *The Genesis of Parliamentary Reform* (London, 1964), p. 265.
60. T. Paine, *The Complete Writings of Thomas Paine*, collected and edited by P. S. Foner, 2 volumes (New York, 1945), pp. 369–75.
61. W. Godwin, *Enquiry Concerning Political Justice* (with selections from Godwin's other writings), abridged and edited by K. Codell Carter (Oxford, 1971), p. 138; emphasis added.
62. Paine, op. cit., p. 341; emphasis added.
63. Godwin, op. cit., pp. 197, 199.
64. Paine, op. cit., pp. 342, 374, 373.

65. Godwin, op. cit., p. 200; emphasis added. Godwin obviously recognised the importance of property in creating and maintaining inequality, but he would not have it forcibly redistributed.
66. Paine, op. cit., pp. 286, 364, 338.
67. Godwin, op. cit., pp. 300, 302; emphasis added.
68. Paine, op. cit., pp. 356, 358. Note Paine's use of the 'chain' analogy here albeit in a secular manner.
69. Godwin, op. cit., p. 226. Paine, op. cit., p. 442.
70. Godwin, op. cit., p. 137. Godwin and Bage did meet on two occasions but they were not close friends.
71. Paine, op. cit., p. 431.
72. Godwin, op. cit., pp. 302, 303.
73. See 'An Occasional Letter on the Female Sex', in Paine, op. cit., pp. 34–8.
74. Ibid., p. 34. This writer recognises the connection between adoration and oppression.
75. Ibid., p. 35.
76. Ibid., p. 36.
77. Veitch, op. cit., p. 326.
78. Ibid., p. 125.
79. Bage could undoubtedly have been more radical on the issue of female emancipation without much fear of persecution.

10: THE EXALTED HEROINE AND THE TRIUMPH OF ORDER

1. A. S. Haskell, 'The Portrayal of Women by Chaucer and his Age', in M. Springer (ed.), *What Manner of Woman* (Oxford, 1978), pp. 1–14, (p. 7).
2. J. J. Richetti, 'The Portrayal of Women in Restoration and Eighteenth Century English Literature', in Springer, op. cit., pp. 65–97, (p. 67).
3. R. J. Clements and J. Gibaldi, *Anatomy of the Novella* (New York, 1977).
4. D. J. Latt, 'Praising Virtuous Ladies: The Literary Image and Historical Reality of Women in Seventeenth-Century England', in Springer, op. cit., pp. 39–64, (pp. 40, 43).
5. I do not argue that this was a unified and concerted strategy, but simply that this view probably appealed to the majority of the bourgeoisie.
6. D. Spearman, *The Novel and Society* (London, 1966), pp. 29–37, 58.

Select Bibliography

BOOKS

Adburgham, A., *Women in Print* (London, 1978).

Allen, W., *The English Novel* (Harmondsworth, 1978).

Avineri, S., *The Social and Political Thought of Karl Marx* (Cambridge, 1968).

Bäckmann, S., *This Singular Tale* (Berlingska, Bocktryckeviet, Lund, 1971).

Bage, R., *Hermsprong, or Man as He is Not*, with an introduction by V. Wilkins (London, 1951).

Ball, D. L., *Samuel Richardson's Theory of Fiction* (The Hague, 1971).

Battestin, M. C., *The Moral Basis of Fielding's Art* (New Haven, Connecticut, 1959).

Benjamin, W., *Illuminations* (London, 1977).

Boswell, J., *The Life of Johnson*, The Penguin English Library (Harmondsworth, 1979).

Burney, F., *Evelina*, edited with an introduction by E. A. Bloom, Oxford English Novels (London, 1968).

Butt, J., *English Literature in the Mid-Eighteenth Century*, edited and completed by G. D. Carnall, The Oxford History of English Literature, 13 volumes (London, 1979), vol. 8.

Cannon, J., Aristocratic Century: The Peerage of Eighteenth-Century England (Cambridge, 1984).

Carpenter, S. C., *Eighteenth-Century Church and People* (London, 1959).

Carroll, J. (ed.), *Selected Letters of Samuel Richardson* (Oxford, 1964).

Clark, J. C. D., *English Society 1688–1832* (Cambridge, 1985).

Clements, R. J., and Gibaldi, J., *Anatomy of the Novella* (New York, 1977).

Collins, A. S., *Authorship in the Days of Johnson* (London, 1927).

Diamond, A., and Edwards., L. R., (eds), *The Authority of Experience: Essays in Feminist Criticism* (Massachusetts, 1977).

Dobson, A., *Fanny Burney* (London, 1903).

Eagleton, T., *The Rape of Clarissa* (Minneapolis, 1986).

Eaves, T. C. D., and Kimpel, B. D., *Samuel Richardson: A Biography* (Oxford, 1971).

Faulkner, P., *Robert Bage*, Twaynes English Authors (Boston, 1979).

Fielding, H., *Amelia*, Everyman's Library (London, 1974).

Fielding, S., *The Adventures of David Simple*, including *Volume the Last*, edited with an introduction by M. Kelsall, Oxford English Novels (London, 1969).

George, M. D., *London Life in the Eighteenth Century* (Harmondsworth, 1964).

Gilbert, A. D., *Religion and Society in Industrial England: Church, Chapel and Social Change* (London, 1976).

Godwin, W., *Enquiry Concerning Political Justice*, with selections from Godwin's other writings, abridged and edited by K. Codell Carter (Oxford, 1971).

Goffman, E., *The Presentation of Self in Everyday Life* (London, 1966).

Goffman, E., *Stigma* (Harmondsworth, 1968).

Goldsmith, O., *The Vicar of Wakefield*, Everyman's Library (London, 1976).

Goldsmith, O., *The Vicar of Wakefield*, edited with an introduction by A. Friedman, Oxford English Novels (London, 1976).

Graves, R., *The Spiritual Quixote*, edited with an introduction by C. Tracy, Oxford English Novels (London, 1967).

Graves, R., *The Spiritual Quixote*, with an introduction by C. Whibley, 2 volumes (London, 1926).

Hemmings, F. W. J. (ed.), *The Age of Realism* (Harmondsworth, 1974).

Hilles, F. W. (ed.), *The Age of Johnson* (New Haven, Connecticut, 1949).

Hopkins, R. H., *The True Genius of Oliver Goldsmith* (Baltimore, 1969).

Jewitt, L. (ed.), *The Life of William Hutton* (London, 1872).

Kelly, G., *The English Jacobin Novel* (London, 1976).

Kinkead-Weekes, M., *Samuel Richardson, Dramatic Novelist* (London, 1973).

Konigsberg, B., *Samuel Richardson and the Dramatic Novel* (Lexington, Kentucky, 1968).

Kreissman, B., *Pamela-Shamela*, University of Nebraska Studies: New Series, 22 (Nebraska, 1960).

Laurenson, D., and Swingewood, A., *The Sociology of Literature* (St Albans, 1972).

Lytton Sells, A., *Oliver Goldsmith: His Life and Works* (London, 1974).

Marx, K., *Capital*, 3 volumes, (London, 1974) vol. 1.

Marx, K., and Engels, F., *The German Ideology*, includes *Introduction to a Critique of Political Economy* (London, 1974).

Mészáros, I., *Marx's Theory of Alienation* (London, 1972).

Miliband, R., *Marxism and Politics*, Marxist Introductions (Oxford, 1977).

Mullan, J., *Sentiment and Sensibility* (Oxford, 1988).

Macpherson, C. B., *The Political Theory of Possessive Individualism* (Oxford, 1962).

McLellan, D. (ed.), *Marx's Grundrisse* (St Albans, 1971).

Needham, G. B., and Utter, R. P., *Pamela's Daughters* (London, 1937).

Neuburg, V., *Popular Literature* (Harmondsworth, 1977).

Opie, I., and Opie, P., *The Classic Fairy Tales* (London, 1980).

Paine, T., *The Complete Writings of Thomas Paine*, collected and edited by P. S. Foner, 2 volumes (New York, 1945).

Paulson, R., *Satire and the Novel in Eighteenth-Century England* (New Haven, Connecticut and London, 1967).

Rawson, C. (ed.), *Henry Fielding*, Penguin Critical Anthologies (Harmondsworth, 1973).

Richardson, S., *Pamela*, Everyman's Library, 2 volumes (London, 1976).

Richetti, J. J., *Popular Fiction Before Richardson* (Oxford, 1969).

Riesman, D., et al., *The Lonely Crowd* (New York, 1953).

Rogers, P., *Henry Fielding: A Biography* (London, 1979).

Rudé, G., *Hanoverian London* (London, 1971).

Scott, W., *Lives of the Novelists* (Oxford, 1906).

Shepherd, T. B., *Methodism and Literature of the Eighteenth Century* (London, 1940).

Smallwood, A. J., *Fielding and the Woman Question* (New York, 1989).

Spacks, P. M., *Imagining a Self* (Massachusetts, 1976).

Spearman, D., *The Novel and Society* (London, 1966).
Springer, M. (ed.), *What Manner of Woman* (Oxford, 1978).
Steeves, H. R., *Before Jane Austen* (London, 1966).
Stone, L., *The Family, Sex and Marriage in England 1500–1800* (Harmondsworth, 1979).
Tawney, R. H., *Religion and the Rise of Capitalism* (Harmondsworth, 1977).
Tompkins, J. M. S., *The Popular Novel in England 1790–1850* (London, 1932).
Tripathi, P. D., *The Doctrinal English Novel* (Calcutta, 1977).
Veitch, G. S., *The Genesis of Parliamentary Reform* (London, 1964).
Walzer, M., *The Revolution of the Saints* (New York, 1974).
Wardle, R. M., *Oliver Goldsmith* (Kansas, 1957).
Watkins, O. C., *The Puritan Experience* (London, 1972).
Watt, I., *The Rise of the Novel* (Harmondsworth, 1972).
Weber, M., *The Protestant Ethic and the Spirit of Capitalism* (London, 1930).
Williams, R., *The Long Revolution* (Harmondsworth, 1965).

JOURNALS

Anon, 'Richard Graves', *Times Literary Supplement*, 11 May 1922, pp. 297–8.
Faulkner, P., 'Man as He is Not', *Durham University Journal*, 1964–5, pp. 137–47.
Hill, C. J., 'The Literary Career of Richard Graves', *Smith College Studies in Modern Languages*, XVI, October 1934 – July 1935, pp. 1–148.
LeGates, M., 'The Cult of Womanhood in Eighteenth-Century Thought', *Eighteenth-Century Studies*, 10, 1976–7, pp. 21–39.
Rymer, M., 'Satiric Technique in *The Spiritual Quixote*', *Durham University Journal*, 65, 1972–3, pp. 54–64.

Index

on H. Fielding's attitude towards
  women, 153 n.3
Smollett, T.
  and Methodism, 98, 158 n.39
  and Goldsmith, 29
social conflict
  causes, 12
  Bage on, 132, 134
social distinctions
  eighteenth-century view, 11
  and Puritanism, 47
  in Bage, 130–1
  in Burney, 118–21
  in Fielding, H., 70–1, 73
  in Fielding, S., 58–9
  in Goldsmith, 82–4
  in Graves, 104, 105
  in Richardson, 41, 47
social integration
  authors view of, 10–11
  individual–society opposition, 7, 10
  in Bage, 32–3, 35
  in Burney, 31, 35
  in Fielding, H., 26–7, 34
  in Fielding, S., 25, 60
  in Goldsmith, 29–30, 35
  in Graves, 28, 34
  in Richardson, 7, 11, 24, 33
social mobility
  in novels, 7–8, 14, 139–40
  Burney and, 35, 118, 121–2
  Fielding, H., and, 71–2
  Fielding, S., and, 33–4
  Goldsmith and, 35
  Graves and, 34
  Richardson and, 24, 33, 39, 42, 47
social origins of authors, 4–5, 19–20, 22
Spacks, P.M.
  on stability of characters in novel,
    46–7
  on Burney, 31
  on Richardson, 43, 140
Spearman, D.
  as critic, 146
spinsters
  economic role of, 13
  and Methodism, 99
  Fielding, S., on, 56, 57, 142
  Bage on, 128
Sterne, L.
  Goldsmith's opinion of, 29
Stone, L.
  on contraception, 127

on individualism, 9; *see also*
  individualism
on mistresses, 44; *see also* adultery
on women and education, 12–13; *see
  also* women and education

Tawney, R.H.
  on individualism, 8, 144; *see also*
    individualism
Tompkins, J.M.S.
  on didacticism, 18, 23; *see also*
    didacticism
  on Bage, 31
  on Richardson, 23
Tracy, C.
  on Graves, 27
Tripathi, P.D.
  on Bage, 134

Veitch, G.S.
  on reform, 138
  on Bage and Godwin, 135

Weber, M.
  on economic individualism and the
    Protestant Ethic, 8; *see also*
    individualism
Walzer, M.
  on poverty, 40; *see also* poor/poverty
  on Puritanism and women, 45; *see
    also* Puritanism
Wardle, R.M.
  on Goldsmith, 28–9
Watt, I.
  on chastity, 42, 140; *see also* chastity
  on individualism and Defoe, 10; *see
    also* individualism
  on individualism and Hume, 147
    n.23; *see also* individualism
  on legal position of women, 48; *see
    also* law/legal reform
  marriage between classes, 71–2; *see
    also* marriage
  on reading public, 21–2; *see also*
    reading public
  on realism, 16–17; *see also* realism
  'sociosomatic snobbery', 65; *see also*
    women, physical constitution
  women and sexuality, 48, 50, 141; *see
    also* women and sexuality
wealth
  in Bage, 132
  in Burney, 121, 122

Index

in Fielding, S., 59, 60
in Goldsmith, 82–3
in Graves, 105, 106
in Richardson, 39–40, 41
Weber, M.
on economic individualism, 8; *see also* individualism
Wesley, J.
and Anglicanism, 97–8; *see also* Anglicanism; Methodism
Whibley, C.
on Graves, 108
Whitefield, G.
Graves on, 98, 100
Wilkins, V.
on Bage, 123, 124, 133, 134
Williams, R.
on authors, 19; *see also* social origins of authors
women, conduct
in novels, 139–47
in Bage, 126–8
in Burney, 35, 110–12, 113–16
in Fielding, H., 64–5
in Fielding, S., 56, 58
in Goldsmith, 76, 77–8
in Graves, 99–101
in Richardson, 48, 49–51, 151 n.54
see also feminine ideal
women and education
and leisure, 13
Bage on, 125–6, 131
Burney on, 116

Fielding, H., on, 63–4, 71
Fielding, S., on, 56
Richardson on, 51
women and equality/emancipation
in novels, 143
Bage on, 123, 124, 125–6, 163 n.79
Fielding, H., on, 153 n.3
Graves on, 101–2
Richardson on, 50–1, 53, 152 nn.56–8, 153 n.3
women, physical constitution
fainting, 100, 158 n.46
in Burney, 111
in Fielding, H., 65, 100
in Goldsmith, 78–9
in Graves, 100
Watt on, 65
women and sexuality
and Puritanism, 50
in sixteenth and seventeenth-century literature, 141
in Fielding, H., 63
in Goldsmith, 78
LeGates on, 13–14
see also feminine ideal; chastity
Work, J.A.
on Fielding, H., 67
working class
as 'mob', 104
women, 13
in Fielding, H., 70
in Graves, 93
Locke on, 9